T0209821

Wherever you are on your path and using Spiritual Response Therapy, this book will certainly engage you and expand your use of the system. Bill takes you through the various levels of interest you may have had when you first learned SRT:

- From understanding what it is like working with Spirit
- To deepening your connection with Spirit by asking questions for clearing
- To expanding your practice for your community and your business

The book is rich with Bill's passion for Co-Creating with Source and it is full of wonderful case studies to bring home the adventure of the healing process.

And, thought someday you might create a business for your own healing practice? Bill shares numerous suggestions of the nuts and bolts of solid business practices such as staffing, accounting and positive connection building for public presentations and social media.

This book is a practical guidepost for applying SRT to your journey!

—Karen Kent, SRT Teacher

When we discover something that fills us with awe and impacts our life positively, we want to share our experience with the world. Such is the nature of this handy little book by Bill Gee. He records his practices step by step as he was setting up his own practices as a healing consultant. This book is for those who have studied Spiritual Response Therapy (SRT) as originally taught by Robert Detzler. Bill generously shares his experience of applying his knowledge and connecting with Spirit to develop a healing service with his wife. It is a simple book, easy to read and full of practical tips and guidance. Recently certified students of SRT will find this book useful.

— Malabika Shaw, SRT Teacher

Conscious Conduit is a valuable, step-by-step resource for those interested in exploring SRT or anyone who would like a stronger relationship with the Divine. Bill provides real-life examples of how to connect to radiant love, heal family dynamics, as well as plenty of practical advice on becoming a happier person as your soul continues on its eternal journey.

— Raven Mardirosian, author of *The Reluctant Tarot Reader*

CONSCOUS
CONDUIT

A USER'S GUIDE TO ASCENSION

WILLIAM GEE

BALBOA.
PRESS

A DIVISION OF HAY HOUSE

Balboa Press books may be ordered through booksellers or by contacting:

Balboa Press
A Division of Hay House
1663 Liberty Drive
Bloomington, IN 47403
www.balboapress.com
1 (877) 407-4847

Because of the dynamic nature of the Internet, any web addresses or links contained in this book may have changed since publication and may no longer be valid. The views expressed in this work are solely those of the author and do not necessarily reflect the views of the publisher, and the publisher hereby disclaims any responsibility for them.

The author of this book does not dispense medical advice or prescribe the use of any technique as a form of treatment for physical, emotional, or medical problems without the advice of a physician, either directly or indirectly. The intent of the author is only to offer information of a general nature to help you in your quest for emotional and spiritual well-being. In the event you use any of the information in this book for yourself, which is your constitutional right, the author and the publisher assume no responsibility for your actions.

Any people depicted in stock imagery provided by Getty Images are models, and such images are being used for illustrative purposes only.

Certain stock imagery © Getty Images.

Scripture texts in this work are taken from the New American Bible, revised edition © 2010, 1991, 1986, 1970 Confraternity of Christian Doctrine, Washington, D.C. and are used by permission of the copyright owner. All Rights Reserved. No part of the New American Bible may be reproduced in any form without permission in writing from the copyright owner.

Print information available on the last page.

ISBN: 978-1-9822-1679-5 (sc)
ISBN: 978-1-9822-1678-8 (e)

Balboa Press rev. date: 11/20/2018

Contents

Introduction

How I Wrote This Book

First, allow me to say right out of the gate that I cannot take full credit for writing this book. SPIRIT channeled each topic in this book. I am merely the conduit.

As my wife, Nina can attest to, whenever I have tried to write about my life story in the past, the writing has been bad. REALLY bad. Before my connection to SPIRIT, my writing came off as pompous, self-serving drivel that was borne from a karmic need to be "right" all the time, even if it meant not speaking "truth". It took a lot of Soul work to let go of that karmic need, and I cannot thank Nina enough for helping me find the path that allowed me to finally let that part of me go.

After I decided to allow SPIRIT to guide what I write and allow myself to be the conduit, my writing has been able to reach its intended audience. The feedback from our clients and the larger Spiritual community has been invaluable as the Work provides the help and insight needed to aid in our collective Ascension.

The intention of this book is to help the new Practitioner of Spiritual Response Therapy (SRT) to navigate their world from a new perspective. When we think about a "user's guide", whether that guide is supposed to tell you how to program your television or the proper way to eat a papaya, what we expect is a manual on the "proper" way to do something. This book is not that type of user's guide. The purpose of this guide is to give you a roadmap you can use to help navigate the strange and wonderful world of SRT, but the ultimate journey and how you get there is for you to decide, not me.

I am assuming that you have already taken the Basic and/or Advanced SRT training, or perhaps you are seriously thinking about it and you want to know a little more about what you might be getting into. It is also possible that you learned SRT on your own by reading Robert's books, and here you may be looking for a little more guidance as to what you should do next. SPIRIT has guided me to write this book for you. With this book, you can learn a little more about how to align your soul to be a clearer conduit for High Self, and then to provide you with a practical guide to turn what you have learned into a successful business where you help others to find the same connection you have.

In addition to writing this book, I also write a weekly blog that I channel with the assistance of SPIRIT and High Self. My original plan was to compile this book into a collection of blog posts, but SPIRIT had other plans, and I am very glad for it.

Before I wrote each chapter of this book, I would begin with my Prep to Work, which we will discuss in a little more detail in Chapter 1, and I ask SPIRIT if it knows what I will be writing. If I have an idea about what the chapter should be about, I will simply ask for some guided "high points" to include. I then turn to the Spiritual Response Therapy (SRT) Charts. Since my ego has been set aside, and before I begin, I often have no idea what we are going to write. I am literally the blank slate upon which SPIRIT can dictate its message. SPIRIT then guides me to three or four charts and I write down what I see. I then look at what SPIRIT has provided and I look for a pattern. Once I see the pattern, I ask SPIRIT to confirm if the pattern I am seeing is what they intend for me to write. Once I get an affirmative of 100%, I get to work.

In the chapters, you will often see citations within the text that refer to certain SRT charts. Those are direct messages from SPIRIT that High Self has asked me to include in the narrative.

As I begin to write, my ego often goes somewhere else as the words start to come out of my keyboard. In a way, I almost feel like the secretary of my High Self, as they tell me what to write. After High Self channels the message, they allow me to come back and edit the passage for those silly things like grammar, flow, and style, but they NEVER allow me to change the direction or the message of the chapter.

This book will not to teach you how to do SRT. Not only are the SRT training materials protected by copyright, the intent of this book is to be merely a supplement to the work of Robert Detzler, the original channel of SRT and the founder of the Spiritual Response Association (SRA). Robert's books are required reading for all SRT Practitioners, Certified Consultants and Teachers, and the copyrighted training materials are only available to those students who are receiving SRT training by a Certified SRT Teacher.

During his life, Robert was constantly channeling new information from High Self and communicating that information through regular communications with the SRT community. Robert passed away in 2013, but even though SRT's primary conduit is no longer with us, SPIRIT continues to work through others to provide the SRT community with new information and insights to Ascension. I am merely one of many as the Work continues to grow and evolve.

Therefore, I dedicate this book to SPIRIT and High Self, from whom this book would not be possible, and to Robert Detzler, to whom the system of SRT would not exist in its present form. I also dedicate this book to myself, High Self's "editor", whose trust and unconditional love for SPIRIT has made this communication possible for you, the student, to gain insight.

Finally, I would like to acknowledge and thank my wife, Nina, and the SRT teachers and practitioners who helped to make this book possible. Words cannot adequately express my gratitude for your patience, your willingness to read my early drafts and provide feedback, and to be a second check with High Self to be sure that the words on these pages come from divine SOURCE, and not my Ego. So thank you, Malabika Shaw, Karen Kent, and Marla Goldberg. Thank you for believing in this project and for believing that I am a worthy conduit for bringing this information to the people who are guided to read it.

PART I

YOUR PERSONAL PATH TO ASCENSION

Chapter 1

Blocks to Our Prep to Work

In our Advanced SRT Procedures Manual, there is a two page procedure describing what most practitioners should use for the Preparation (Prep) to Work before they start working with the pendulum on a Client. SPIRIT assures me that the procedure described is 100% effective if used with the correct intention. You can even "train" your soul to complete the Prep to Work in a matter of seconds if you do the work often enough.

However, for some practitioners, despite completing the Prep to Work procedures as prescribed, they still have difficulty remaining connected to SPIRIT while they work, and often feel as though they have to start all over again.

SPIRIT informs me that there are three common issues that block a practitioner's Prep to Work. These are 1) Discordant Energies (Charts 6a & 5), 2) Final Assurance (Chart 25), and 3) Blocks that are preventing your High Self Committee from operating from the New Paradigm above RADIANT LOVE (Charts 3 & 18).

The specific Discordant Energies that tend to interfere with a practitioner's prep to work are Excesses, Self-Limitation and Ego. If we combine all three of these discordant energies together, what we generally have is a practitioner who lacks self-confidence that they can make a strong connection to SPIRIT. The Ego is the part of us that is firmly rooted in the physical plane of existence, and therefore it has a great deal of difficulty seeing anything beyond what it can touch, taste or smell. Therefore, the ego tends to rely too heavily on sensory input. This tends to lean it towards excess. Meanwhile, the ego tends to disbelieve anything it cannot actually experience in a physical way.

How we deal with these particular discordant energies is that we must address the ego directly whenever we are doing the Work of SRT. We must reduce the influence of the ego to less than 3%. We cannot reduce the ego all the way down to 0% because the ego is still necessary for your physical vessel to operate. We can reduce the ego nearly to zero while in deep meditation, but that requires a disconnection to sensory input almost to the point of a deep sleep, which is not practical when we are working with a client. However, since it is possible to reduce its influence, we can then clear the discordant energies so we can get back to the Work.

If simply reducing the ego does not work, then something else is informing the ego to remain strong during the session. SPIRIT informs me that when the ego refuses to be reduced during the Prep to Work, then it is likely that some outside interference is influencing it. Specifically, SPIRIT directs me to "Dark Forces" on Chart 5.

When we think of Dark Forces, what SPIRIT is referring to is the drive we have within all of us to seek answers inside "dual space", which is the realm of the ego. That is, our disconnection with SOURCE drives us to see the world in terms of "good and evil", "black and white", and so on. The problem, of course, is that duality is an illusion that the ego created due to its inability to connect to SOURCE energy. Further, our culture has indoctrinated us to see the world in dualistic terms, which builds up the ego while at the same time, it enforces our disconnection with SPIRIT.

With your pendulum, clear the influence of Dark Forces from your ego, and then repeat the procedure of reducing the ego to less than 3%.

The second common block to our Prep to Work is on Chart 25, "Guarantee that Everything is Cleared". As the channel for SPIRIT, your energy must be as clear as possible in order for the ego to not re-assert itself into your session. We do this by providing SPIRIT with final assurance that whatever programs and other energetic "baggage" you brought with you before you began the Work is clear, and to seal that clearing with a guarantee that nothing will come up during the session that does not belong to the client you are working with.

This can be a challenge due to our old friend, the ego. When I started to do SRT clearings professionally, I was the type of practitioner who loved to tell stories from my own life that I felt was relevant to whatever the client was going through. What I believed I was doing was by providing an example of a similar drama in my own life; I was providing my client with some context. The problem with this approach was that the only person seeking "context" was me and my own ego and not my client. By bringing up the stories about me, all I was doing was exploring my own programs that I needed to work on rather than focusing on the needs of my client. While I was not necessarily neglecting the needs of my client, I did end up spending just as much time clearing my client's programs as I was clearing my own programs. The problem with this approach, of course, is that your client is paying you to address their programs and issues, not your own.

While there is breath in our bodies, we will continue to have programs to clear. After all, that is the whole point of our physical existence in the first place! However, when you are the Practitioner and you are working on a client, it is important that you set aside all of that and put all of your attention on your client's needs and set your own needs aside, at least for the time being. Whether your client is someone who is paying you for your services or whether it is a member of your family or circle of friends, you have a professional obligation to keep your ego in check. If something comes up during the session that reminds you of a program you need to clear in yourself, make a note of it and come back to it later when you give yourself time for self-care.

The third common block to our Prep to Work has to do with our High Self committee. The Prep to Work materials from the Spiritual Response Association reads as follows:

> Verify the level of consciousness of your High Self committee. Turn to Chart 3, and ask "What is the lowest level consciousness of any member of my High Self committee; is the level on the first page OR the second page of Chart 3?" You may turn the chart sideways on the indicated side to find the exact level using the pendulum.

> If the level is anything other than the highest level on the second page of Chart 3, (well above the words "RADIANT LOVE" as printed on the chart), ask SPIRIT to "Please clear, remove, elevate and educate committee members to the highest level on Chart 3." Then recheck the

level: "Is my High Self committee cleared to the Heart of SPIRIT and the highest level of RADIANT LOVE?"

Verify that all your spiritual committees including Guardian Angels are at the highest level of RADIANT LOVE on Chart 3.

So what happens when you follow the above protocol and some or none of your High Self Committees are able to elevate to the level above RADIANT LOVE? I have found that not being at RADIANT LOVE at the Level of 1st Expression side of Chart 3 is where these souls in your committee are generally finding themselves stuck. When clearing Chart 3, Robert would sometimes be very specific when it came to the exact location of where the committees were stuck and sometimes he was not. If SPIRIT is guiding you to a specific area on Chart 3 where your committees are stuck, then work to determine the nature of the blockage using charts 5, 6a, 6b, 18, etc. Otherwise, simply use the phrase, "Please clear, remove, elevate and educate committee members to the highest level on Chart 3", and then recheck the level by saying "is my High Self Committee clear to the Heart of SPIRIT and the highest level of RADIANT LOVE?"

For example, when doing my prep to work for this chapter, I found my High Self Committee blocked at the Lord/1st Eden level on Chart 3. It is at this stage of a soul's development, before it begins its journey on the physical plane, where we have the nearly countless choices of life patterns to follow in order to learn the lessons we need to learn so we can connect to SOURCE. SOURCE provides the millions of choices as a set of instructions for each soul to complete before the soul can ascend back to itself. In order to move the soul to the next level, the soul will need to overcome each embedded block within each of the millions of possible life choices. SPIRIT informs me that in this context, "Blocks from God Over Sun" (Chart 18) was the appropriate mechanism by which these blocks on the 900 million paths had taken place.

So in order to elevate these members of my High Self committee, I had to ask: "Are any members of my High Self committee blocked at the 'Lord/1st Eden' level on Chart 3 due to 'Blocks from God Over Sun'"? I received a "yes" response, so I asked High Self to clear those blocks to open the door to elevate those members of my High Self committee to the highest level on Chart 3. I then repeated the protocol until my High Self committee was above RADIANT LOVE and received 100% assurance that all members of my High Self committee was operating at the highest possible vibration.

After you have been practicing SRT for a while, your Prep to Work ritual will take less and less time. Most experienced practitioners are able to complete the Prep to Work in a matter of seconds, but we must NEVER skip or assume that the Prep to Work phase is complete unless it we do it consciously and with intention. As a reinforcement practice, try to go through the entire Prep to Work procedure at least once per month. That way, should your ego try to assert itself or if members of your High Self committee find themselves where they do not belong, you can address those issues without any issues for your clients.

Chapter 2

Pendulum Wise

As SRT Practitioners, our physical bodies are the "tool" that SPIRIT uses to communicate, but the primary amplification tool we use to connect with SPIRIT and High Self is the pendulum. While some practitioners like their pendulums to reflect their own sense of aesthetic, in order for a pendulum to function, it only needs to be a weight on the end of a string or chain. It is important that the pendulum fits comfortably in your hand and the weight is not to light or too heavy. Generally, the weight should be no more than half an ounce (15 grams), and no less than a tenth of an ounce (5 grams). Personally, I prefer a pendulum right in the middle of that range that is three tenths of an ounce (10 grams).

What materials compose the pendulum also depends on the personal taste of the user and what the intended purpose of pendulum. For general SRT work, I find it is usually best to use inert materials such as glass, plastic, sterling silver and stainless steel, rather than using precious or semi-precious stones or gems. Other forms of energy work, will call for a pendulum containing a magnet or containing a stone that will clear specific physical ailments from the body, but I generally do not use those pendulums for SRT research.

If you have spent some time working with your pendulum, you may have a favorite you like to use, or you may have a small collection of all different types and styles depending on your mood for that day or the personal taste of your client. A tarot reader friend of mine allows their client to choose the deck they want to use for their reading. If you have a wide variety of pendulum styles, you may want to allow them to choose which pendulum they want you to use. It should not make any difference in the quality of the reading, but it will allow the client to feel more invested in the process, and perhaps that will make them feel more open to what you have to say.

The length of the chain is also a matter of taste rather than functionality. A short chain will give you a rapid swing, and it may be easier to see subtle changes in its direction. A long chain will give you a longer, more deliberate swing, and it makes it easier for you to attach a clasp so you can wear the pendulum as a bracelet or necklace. This can be especially convenient if you are the type of person who has a tendency to drop or misplace things.

Some users report that their pendulums have different personalities and preferences, but I would caution you not to give the pendulum more power by treating it like a person. SPIRIT does not inhabit your pendulum; SPIRIT works through you and the pendulum is merely the tool by which SPIRIT is communicating. When we assign our tools a "personality", what this will sometimes lead to are disincarnates attempting to inhabit a pendulum in an attempt to communicate or otherwise influence the reading. This is why it is very important that you clear your tools as frequently as possible. I use is a block of selenite that is kept in the same place I store my pendulums, but you can also ask High Self to clear your tools each time you use them.

Therefore, beyond SRT, SPIRIT informs me that the pendulum is an excellent tool to help you navigate your everyday life. SRT does not come with a vow of poverty! If your health or financial security is preventing you from doing the Work, then your High Self wants you to get those things taken care of. You can use your pendulum for "security, resources; money, income;" and "health, fitness" (Chart 2). The reason why SPIRIT encourages you to use the pendulum in this manner is because SPIRIT needs you to be the channel for High Self, and you have "lessons to accomplish before moving on, working with ONE" (Chart 20). That is what drew you to SRT in the first place and so that is the reason why doing the work is so important.

The biggest challenge with using the pendulum to increase your own health and prosperity is getting over our old friend, the ego. Remember, the ego is a selfish, apathetic, and rarely satisfied entity, so the ego has no place when it comes to increasing one's prosperity and health. The ego sees the world through the lens of the "zero-sum game". The zero-sum game is the paradigm dominant in Western cultures, which tells us that in order for one person to be successful, someone else must fail. Fortunately, for us, the zero-sum game is yet another illusion created by the ego when the truth is the Universe contains all of the energy and resources for everyone to live their lives to their fullest potential and we need only tap into that potential while being guided by High Self!

Therefore, before we start dowsing the pendulum at our everyday problems, we must first do our Prep to Work and reduce the influence of the ego to less than 3%. Once complete, then you can ask High Self to guide you to whatever you need to live your most prosperous life!

Use #1: Making good Food Choices

Let us say you are at the grocery store and you are trying to plan meals that are healthy but will taste good at the same time. A friend recommends that you try eating a kale salad, but you have never had a kale salad before and so you do not know how your body will react to it. Clear your mind and break out your pendulum. (Find a private space to do this if you are concerned about people staring at you!)[1]

Ask High Self the percentage of benefit you will derive by eating the kale salad. Since most people do not bring their SRT charts with them to the grocery store, imagine a number chart sitting just above your pendulum with the extreme left being 0% and the extreme right being 100%. If you get a result that is greater than 80%, ask High Self the percentage of enjoyment you will derive by eating the kale salad. If you get a result of over 80%, then you should try the bitter greens. If you get a result of less than 80%, first ask if you have any programs or blocks that are preventing you from deriving the maximum benefit from this food, and if you get a "yes" response, go home and research and clear those programs before going back to the store. If you get a "no" response, then SPIRIT has just informed you that your specific body type will not derive a

---

[1] Personally, I generally do not care if people see me using my pendulum in public. It may even start a conversation that could lead to a new client, but if you are concerned that other people's energy will influence your connection to High Self, by all means, seek a private place to do your Work.

strong benefit and/or enjoyment from that particular food item, and you can now move on to something else.[2]

This method not only works for grocery shopping, you can use it in restaurants or even selecting items from a take-out menu. If you are faced with no food choices above 80%, there is an energetic "life hack" you can try to raise the vibration of the food you are eating that we will describe in more detail in Chapter 3.

Use #2: Buying Supplements and Maximizing Medical Advice

Your medical professional has recommended that you take a certain supplement or herb in order to address a specific condition you happen to be dealing with, but when you get to the supplement isle at your local health food store, there are too many choices and you have no idea which one you should take. Do you go with the inexpensive store brand, or do you take the most expensive brand thinking that if it costs more, then it must be the highest quality? And what about the supplement blends? Just because a blend contains the supplement you need, is it better to take it along with all the other supplements it contains or do you need to stick with the single note supplement your doctor recommended? Is the supplement your doctor recommended even the one you need or is there a different one that is even better? This can be a very confusing and frustrating process, especially if you are not sure

---

[2] With the prevalence of food allergies in today's world, your High Self may be trying to warn you that you may have an allergic reaction to a certain food no matter how "good for you" it is purported to be. Listen to your High Self if it tells you to stay away from a certain food item.

what you should be taking. You could ask your doctor for help, but sometimes they will simply tell you to go with what feels right to you, so all you have left is to ask High Self to help you clear this up!

Just as with the first use above, you complete your Prep to Work and you ask High Self to guide you to the correct supplement that will give you the greatest benefit. Whenever faced with multiple shelves of the same or similar supplements, I first ask High Self to tell me which shelf it is on. Then I ask if it is on the left, right or in the middle. I will then pick up each bottle and ask, "Is this the one?" If I get a "no", I move on to the next until I get a "yes" response. I then ask for a percentage of confirmation that the bottle I have in my hand is the one that I need. If I get a 100% response, I put the bottle into my shopping cart.

Sometimes I am surprised to find the pendulum telling me that none of the supplements my doctor recommended were going to be good for me. In cases like that, I would first ask whether I can find the same type of supplement at another store or if I would need to order it online. If I get a negative response, I would then ask High Self whether there was something completely different that I should try instead.[3] If I get a "yes" response, I would repeat the technique above until I was holding the bottle of whatever High Self was guiding me to. If the bottle I am holding is completely different from what my doctor recommended, I snap a picture of the bottle with

---

[3] Whenever High Self guides you to go against your medical professional's advice, ALWAYS seek confirmation from either the medical professional who gave you that advice or seek a second opinion from a different medical professional. Herbs and supplements are sometimes contraindicated with certain medications or with each other, which can be dangerous if taken in combination without the supervision of someone trained in the medical arts.

my smart phone and I text or email my medical professional asking them if it was okay if I took that supplement instead.

I had a client who was suffering from a chronic condition and was finding no relief from any of the medication his doctor recommended. The client was also taking several supplements that did not seem to be working either. What we did was we went to our local health food store and we used the preceding technique to search for a supplement that would help him. At first, we went to the supplements used to treat my client's condition, and when I received "no" responses for everything on the shelf, I then asked High Self to expand our search to something else. To my surprise, High Self guided me to a supplement that was used to treat a completely different condition.

After consulting with my client's health professional, they felt that there was no risk for the client to try the supplement, and after taking the new supplement for about a week my client experienced immediate relief from his symptoms! After further research, his health professional discovered that the supplement was only useful for my client's specific condition in 5% of all cases, but for that 5%, the supplement was very effective. Of course, this information did not appear on the bottle, but with High Self guiding our efforts, we were able to spare my client a costly trial-and-error process, which may have never led to the right supplement at all!

Use #3: Helping with Other Life Choices

We need a certain amount of material comfort in order for us to do our Work, but often we are faced with choices that appear to be equally good or equally bad that it sometimes feels like we are rolling the dice with life rather than making the right choices that will be in our highest good.

Do I take the job at Company A or Company B? Do I live in a new house in the suburbs or do I buy a fixer-upper in the country? Do I buy the minivan or the sedan? These types of decisions may seem mundane to some people, but for others they can cause a great deal of anxiety, especially because once the decision is made, it can be very difficult to take it back. Of course, you want to make a rational choice when it comes to these sorts of decisions, but as I like to tell my Economics students, human beings are NOT rational creatures! So why should we not turn to High Self for help when we need it?

Whenever you have a difficult life choice in front of you, it is always a good idea to break out the pendulum, but you need to first check in to see how much of your ego is invested in the outcome of the decision.[4] You must reduce your ego to less than 3% or you may have a difficult time making a choice that is in your highest good. If you ego cannot, before you ask the question, you should call in some help from another SRT practitioner or if one is not available, pick a seer who uses a modality you trust. It is important that whomever you call to provide assistance does not have any personal stake in the outcome of the decision you are trying to make. For example, if your seer is your best friend who would be personally hurt if you moved to another part of the country, then perhaps asking them to check with High Self as to whether you should take a job several hundred miles away is not the best idea. If you hand the pendulum to your teenage daughter when you are trying to

---

[4]   In some cases, reducing the ego when making a major life decision may be impossible, especially when the decision involves bringing something we think we *want* into our life verses something we actually *need*.

decide what kind of car to buy, you may find yourself buying the expensive sports car when all you really needed was a sedan! Just as with the supplement example, do not be surprised if the decision High Self directs you to is no decision at all. For example, if you are trying to decide which car to buy, High Self may say that now is not the right time to be buying a car. You may be trying to decide between two possible job offers and High Self directs you to reject both offers and hold out for a third offer that has not presented itself yet. If High Self is not giving you the answer you want to hear, then you simply have to accept that any decision at all is not in your highest good. You may have more programs to clear before the path before you is open enough to allow your greatest destiny to present itself. If that is the case and you attempt to use your will power to get the pendulum to give you an answer, then your ego has taken over and any answer from that point you should not take seriously.

Before we close this chapter, you must remember that in all decision scenarios where you are asking High Self to indicate which decision is in your highest good, you should not to second-guess the decision. High Self loves you and wants you to be successful, so the decision is coming directly from SOURCE. It is like if God Himself has called you on the phone and told you what to do. If God told you to pick door #3, would you then hesitate and pick door #2 instead? I would certainly hope not, but you would be surprised at how many people do just that!

Therefore, any and all second-guessing is being done by your disappointed ego and NOT High Self. If your High Self tells you to eat the kale salad and you decide to eat a cheeseburger instead, your ego has won, and there WILL be consequences. If your High Self tells you to take a specific herb

Chapter 3

Energizing with SPIRIT

As we learned in the preceding chapter, when life presents us with choices, SRT and the pendulum is an excellent tool to find the right choice that is in line with our highest good. Unfortunately, life does not always present us with good choices. Sometimes, circumstances occur where no "good" options exist. What do we do in those types of situations?

Before we were born, our souls selected a life that would present us with experiences that would help us learn the lessons we needed to learn in order to know and appreciate the pure love and light of SOURCE energy. Often that involves experiencing the polar opposite of love and acceptance. When you began the process of clearing those programs and lessons from your soul records using SRT, some of those unpleasant experiences either reduced in intensity or went away altogether. However, since we are all still here in this physical existence, there are likely still things for us to learn, clear, and grow with, otherwise we would have ascended at this point and we would no longer be on this plane.

People and situations surround us in our lives that we feel we cannot change. Our parents are still our parents and our siblings and cousins are still the people they are. Our genetic profile, race, gender and sexual orientation are still the same as they were before we started this process and we still have to live on a planet that is in a constant state of change. If those people and situations in your life were causing you distress before, it is likely that they are still causing you distress now, even if that distress is to a lesser degree thanks to the clearings you received.

SPIRIT informs me that the way to deal with those life situations we cannot change is to raise their energetic vibration so that it is more in tune with SOURCE than it was before. We do this through "clearing statements" and "drawing in Energy" (Chart 19) in order to prevent our worldly "commitments becoming vows" (Chart 24), which would result in our "loss of Spiritual Sight" (Chart 16).

The three major categories we will cover in this chapter are how to raise the vibrational energies surrounding Family, Food and the Environment.

Family

Like it or not, we all have families that we have to deal with on some level. Families are the people in your life that you love, hate, wish you were closer to or wish they were dead, oftentimes all in the same moment! As you live and grow throughout your life, close friends and even spouses can come and go, but your family is here to stay whether you want them to or not. Even those of us who are adopted children or who spent their formative years as wards of the State still had mothers and fathers and adopted family groups to deal with, even if we did not know them all that well.

Since souls tend to travel in packs, your families are often members of your soul group as you have shared dozens, if not hundreds, of lifetimes with them. As such, each of your family members possesses a level of intimate knowledge about who you are and what you have done in your previous lifetimes. Some of those memories are heroic tales of love overcoming impossible odds, and some you would rather cast into the fires of eternity. Your family is your harshest judge as they are often a reflection of your own karmic burdens.

Vast distances and divergent interests cannot cut the ties of family as they are a part of you as much as you are a part of them. If discordant energies between family members are not resolved in this lifetime, you will need to deal with them the next lifetime, or the lifetime after that, or the lifetime after that. Since there is no way to escape this, your only alternative is to raise the vibration of your family relationship, at least insofar as it relates to your own karma and your own programs.

SPIRIT informs me that most of the issues we have with our families are a reflection of the issues and programs we are dealing with ourselves. Therefore, the first step when it comes to raising the vibration of your relationship with your family is to first work on clearing any and all past, present and future life programs having to deal with them. For this work, you may want to seek out the assistance of another SRT Practitioner rather than try to deal with this by yourself. The reason for this is that it is very difficult to approach family issues from a neutral perspective where you can keep your ego at less than 3% influence, especially in cases where present life circumstances involve abuse, trauma, or tragic events.

After clearing all programs to 100%, raise the vibration of your relationship by drawing in the light and love of SOURCE energy and to repeat clearing statements that releases you from any and all karmic ties to these people. Part of that process is forgiving yourself for all past transgressions, even when they were committed in other lifetimes, but it also involves forgiving them for their transgressions towards you, no matter how "unforgiveable" their sins happen to have been. Nobody is perfect, especially not you and me. When Jesus said "Let him who is without sin among you be the first to throw a stone," (John 8:7) he was alluding to the fact that all of us carry the weight of our sins with us throughout all of our lifetimes, and to deny forgiveness and mercy to others is to deny forgiveness and mercy towards ourselves.

The second step when it comes to dealing with family is to try not to "fix" them. Yes, you have found this wonderful energetic healing modality called SRT that can clear all SPIRIT level programs from the beginning of time, but unless your family members WANT to be cleared and they trust you enough to facilitate the clearing, it is not going to happen. Of course, you can ask their High Selves if it is acceptable to clear programs without their conscious permission, but it has been my experience that programs have a tendency to re-assert themselves unless the person receiving the clearing has made a conscious choice to life a life that is free of their programs. The exception to that has been in cases where the cleared programs had to do with the client's relationship with the family member, but even then, we are not trying to change or clear the family member; we are only clearing the energetic programs between the client and the family member.

Over the past ten years, the elderly mother of a client of mine has been a permanent resident in my client's household. As with most people her age, my client's mother suffers from a variety of ailments including slowly progressing dementia. Even though my client tries to get her the care she needs, she generally does not trust doctors nor does she trust alternative healers. My client has been seeing excellent results from her sessions with me, but when she wanted to bring her mother to see me, her mother immediately dismissed me as a "voodoo healer", despite her acknowledgement that her daughter has been doing much better under my care. Further, since the very suggestion of seeing an energy worker seemed to go against her mother's belief systems, it created a further rift between them that they are still trying to work out.

This rift was creating discordant energy between my client and her mother. Therefore, we decided that instead of focusing our efforts on trying to clear her mother's programs, we would instead focus on clearing the relationship itself. What we found were several lifetimes where my client has refused the help her mother had offered her, and other lifetimes where she deliberately hurt her mother because she disagreed with what her mother believed. We then cleared those programs between them so that my client could more readily accept her mother for who she is, this allowed her to honor whatever process her mother's soul had chosen for this particular lifetime.

I am happy to report that since we were able to clear the programs and karma between them, the relationship with my client and her mother has improved greatly. While her mother remains as stubborn and difficult as ever, our ability to release the discordant energy between them has allowed my client to have enough compassion that she can support her mother's own process, even if she continues to disagree with how her mother is doing it.

Food

In the previous chapter, we discussed using the pendulum to make better nutritional choices when we are grocery shopping or even when making choices on a menu at a restaurant. However, what do we do in those circumstances where we have no control over the menu? Whether you are at a dinner party, staying with friends or family, or attending a holiday gathering, sometimes the food choices presented to us are less than ideal. It gets even more challenging if we happen to be living in an assisted living situation, or if we are an inpatient at a hospital, if we are attending a summer camp, or (God forbid) we happen to be incarcerated or living in an institution! How does one take a plate of overcooked canned green beans, French fries and some sort of "mystery meat" and change it into food that nourishes our mind, body and Spirit?

Further, with food choices a grocery stores being limited to genetically-modified, pesticide-laden food-like products, even when it appears we have a choice of what foods we can eat, it is often unavoidable that we are eating substances that could be harming our bodies.

SPIRIT informs me that even when our food choices are limited, we can still derive the maximum vibrational energy from what we eat in exactly the right proportions for our bodies to consume. We do this by downloading all of Chart 9a, "Minerals and Vitamins", into food presented to us in exactly the right proportions that our physical bodies require.

All religious traditions contain one or more blessings related to the food we eat. The idea is to infuse the food with the energetic vibration of the deity so that whoever consumes the food will perform their labors while embodying its holy presence. However, if the food has no nutritional value, or if those who imbibe are made weak or sick from its consumption, then the blessing has no value to anyone unless the required nutrition is included in the blessing.

It is also possible to download certain vitamins and minerals into your body without consuming the foods that contain it. For example, one of our female clients needed to increase her consumption of calcium she was undergoing hormone changes related to the onset of perimenopause. Calcium is best absorbed in the body when combined with magnesium. Unfortunately, the quantity of calcium and magnesium the client needed to consume was hard on her digestive tract and so she ended up not taking the recommended dose due to the discomfort and inconvenience it caused. What my we recommended instead was that our client adjust her supplement intake to a level her stomach could tolerate and we used the pendulum to download the rest from SPIRIT. Six months later when her client went back for her follow up with her doctor, her tests indicated that her calcium levels were exactly where they needed to be![5]

The key to success in raising the vibration of the foods you consume is consistency, trust, and frequency. Do everything in your power to consume only those foods that already contain high vibrational energy, but even the very best food can use a boost of SPIRIT energy in order to maximize the benefit to your body and soul.

---

[5]   As was stated in the previous chapter, whenever attempting to download supplements or dietary recommendations using SRT, it is important that you inform your medical professional and work with them to monitor your progress and make adjustments where needed.

The Environment

Whether we believe that our warming planet is man-made or due to some other forces beyond our control, the fact of the matter is that Climate Change is upon us as average global temperatures continue to break records, extreme weather events have become more frequent and ocean levels continue to rise. The toll that this is going to take on the resources of future generations is almost impossible to imagine. I believe that something we can all agree on is that any attempt to turn back the clock to return the Earth to a time before humanity existed is not realistic.

Rather than attempting to turn back the clock, SPIRIT informs me that we can work to raise the vibration of our environment while at the same time we raise the vibration of our own energies in order that we may be more in harmony with the changes that are occurring. We have to remember that the Earth is always changing, and life on this planet has had to change with it through the ages. Therefore, the bottom line is that as the environment continues to change, we need to be able to adapt!

Adaptation often involves what can appear to be common sense choices, which often have painful emotional consequences. If you live near the coast or a flood plain, you need to move to higher ground. If you live in an area that is turning into a desert, you either need to learn how to live in the desert or move to a place that gets more rainfall. If you live in a densely populated area where food resources are scarce, you will need to help find creative ways to generate more food close to the people who need it or move somewhere where food resources are more plentiful. Clear any attachments that you have to the way things were in the past because they are just that, attachments to an idea or program that are no longer applicable to what is actually happening. It is really that simple.

While you are at it, increase your energetic awareness of the environment around you, and use your pendulum to raise the vibration of the land so that your energy and the energy of the Earth are in harmony with each other. Spend as much time as you can in your natural surroundings, whether those surroundings are a wooded area near your house or a city park in your neighborhood. Ask the land what it needs and use your charts to interpret the results. Then do everything you can to follow the instructions given to you. By doing this, you will find that it will not matter wherever you happen to be in the world, you will have the ability to change your environment so that it is more conducive to your highest good.

On the DNA level, ask High Self to activate your genes and chromosomes that will allow you to adapt to the changing environment, and ask that the activation be passed down to subsequent generations. Within each of our genes are not only the blueprints to adapt to any environmental change that could happen on the Earth, it also contains the ability to communicate and connect to SOURCE energy. The only thing that is preventing our evolution is our own egos and our own inability to let go of dualistic conscious control. If we expand our awareness to the cosmos beyond, and reach out to every entity in the galaxy with love in your heart, we have the ability to ask for whatever assistance we can get to help humanity with the changes that we are adapting to.

SPIRIT has given us the tools we need so we do not lose our Spiritual Sight in the face of those things we think are beyond our control. For too many generations humanity has spent too much of their energy looking backward and getting caught up in worldly commitments that became vows so that we lost sight of SOURCE energy. Nevertheless, the world continues to give us soul families to care for, food to nourish our bodies, and a world to make all of that possible that can be improved and enhanced simply by raising our energetic vibration. The belief that we have no control over any of that is part of the illusion that was designed to bring us back to SOURCE, if we have the courage to see past the illusion and work to reconnect to it.

Chapter 4

Building Stronger Relationships

The process of Spiritual growth can be a long and difficult struggle, which we can make easier or harder depending on the strength of our relationships both inside and outside of our families. A close partner, whether this is a spouse, lover, or best friend can be your greatest ally in this process or they can be your greatest obstacle. In this chapter, we will explore how we can strengthen the relationship with your primary partner so that you have the support you need as you work to clear your programs so that you can get closer to ascension.

Nina and I have been married for nearly 25 years and I will be the first to say that maintaining a long-term relationship can be extremely challenging at times. We are very fortunate that we see each other as partners in our life's journey, even though we are different people who are on somewhat different life paths. From the very beginning of our long history together, we made the conscious choice that we would both be seeking a Spiritual path in life and we agreed that we would support each other in that endeavor no matter how difficult that path got. I strongly believe that our commitment to walk this path together is the main reason why we are still together today mostly because walking the path of SPIRIT is the most important thing we do in our lives.

It is actually rare in the spiritual community to find people who are still in successful long-term relationships that predated their induction into Spirituality. Most of my colleagues who are active seekers are either divorced, in the process of getting divorced, single, or they are divorced and are recently re-married. There are many very successful married couples who are also Spiritual healers, but even these people tend to be on their second or third marriages as their first marriages could not survive the strain of one person seeking the Spiritual path and the other remaining firmly rooted on the physical path.

As you already are aware, following a spiritual path for the first time can be very stressful, especially if up to this point in your life, you allowed your ego to guide your actions. If your partner does not choose to either support nor join you on the spiritual path, they may be choosing to compromise the strength of the intimacy you may have experienced before. If your partner is happy living their lives the same way they always have while you move on to seek a more spirit-minded path, it is likely that they will start to feel like an echo of the person you were, and not the person you are becoming. Therefore, if you feel like you have had a good thing going with your current partner and you do not want to lose that, you need to do everything you can to get them to join you on this journey or you will risk losing the relationship.

SPIRIT informs me that the basis for all strong, Spirit-minded relationships is when both partners agree that "the Intention is Growth" (Chart 27) and that this intention is set from the very beginning of the relationship on both sides. If one partner intends to grow spiritually while the other is perfectly content with everything staying the same, it creates a situation where "Dysfunction of Expression" (Chart 11) is taking place where eventually the two partners grow apart to the point where "Affection and Love" (Chart 2), is no longer possible.

Maintaining the intention of growth in a relationship is not easy. SPIRIT warns that too often when it comes to relationships, there is a danger of "Commitments becoming Vows" (Chart 24) in addition to the stress of "World Energies (Positive and Negative)" and "Polarity Beliefs" (Chart 10a) getting in the way of that growth. Our culture places an enormous amount of pressure on families to act a certain way in order to be "acceptable", while at the same time we restrict their ability to grow spiritually by economic and social constraints. It is hard enough just to pay the bills from month to month, as the demands of work, family and society are ripping us in all different directions at once. Spiritual growth can only happen from a place of silence, so it is no wonder that those of us who seek the Spiritual path are often doing it alone even if we are technically married.

Set the Intention

As a Spiritual Counselor, relationship counseling is one of the most common issues I deal with when working with clients. Whether the client is single and is looking for that perfect partner, or whether the client is in a long-term relationship and cannot understand where the magic has gone, I often find myself counseling relationships that are at one or more stages of crisis. In almost all cases, when these people first went out into the world to find their life partner, what they failed to do from the beginning was to set the right intention for the relationship.

If you are not currently in a relationship and would like to find that special someone, your first critical step is to set the intention for growth. Send the energy out into the Universe that what you need is a partner who is also on a Spiritual path and is working towards ascension. You may not think they exist or you may believe that all the "good ones" are already taken, but as humanity begins to become more and more self-aware, odds are your future partner is closer than you think! All you have to do is believe it and let the Universe know that you are ready.

If there is something inside of you that cannot be convinced that you can find the right partner who is on the same path that you are, it is possible that you are running one or more programs from other lifetimes that are getting in the way. You can clear those programs yourself or you can seek out a healer to do it for you, and then work to set your intention again.

Once you find a person that you think may be right for you, make sure that you connect on a Spiritual as well as a physical level. Just because you set the intention and somebody shows up, does not necessarily mean that they are the person you are looking for. If you do not feel 100% confident that this person is on the same path as you, check with High Self[6] and talk it out with your prospective partner. If they are on the same page with you, it should be obvious.

If you are already in a relationship and you are worried that the original intention that got you together was not right, it may not be too late to establish a new intention. Even if you have been married for several years, but you are afraid that the

---

[6]   It may be a good idea to ask a friend to assist with the research or go and see a Practitioner you trust rather than attempting to throw the pendulum yourself. New relationships make the ego REALLY happy and so you may not be able to reduce its influence to the point where you get accurate results.

relationship is in crisis, some degree of "couples counseling" may be what you need, It is possible that at the beginning of the relationship the two of you were on the same page together but then "life got in the way" and now you are moving on divergent paths.

If you can find a way to get back on the same path together, then the relationship may yet work out for the long term. However, if you cannot seem to get on the same page, then sometimes separation, divorce or just splitting up is the only option available to you, but I would try to avoid that alternative until you are absolutely certain that things are not going to work out. If there is no hope for your current relationship, then once it is over, be sure to set the right intention for the next relationship.

Too often, couples stay together for the wrong reasons that have nothing to do with the strength of the relationship itself. These reasons can include children, financial stability, traditional family beliefs, political appearances, or any other of the thousands of reasons grounded in social norms that have everything to do with the ego and dualistic thinking while ignoring the spiritual well-being of the souls who are feeling trapped in a relationship that is not working for them. From the moment you decide that walking away from a long-term relationship is one option available to you, it is amazing at how many new options and lines of communication are opened up that may save your current relationship.

Perhaps the Universe intended that you need to walk your personal soul journey alone. Some of the greatest spiritual people of all time did not have long-term relationships with anyone except SPIRIT and their community of like-minded people. If that is your path, do not feel bad that you will not be sharing an intimate relationship with another person. Feel joyous that you have the opportunity to share your journey with your entire community!

Blocks to Successful Relationships

Even when the intention for Spiritual growth was set from the beginning of the relationship, people can change over time. Life is full of challenges, drama, scarcity and pain, which can put a strain on even the strongest relationships.

One of the biggest challenges we have in our physical manifestation is our separation from SOURCE energy by the ego, which is rooted in dualistic beliefs. Remember that the ego is an apathetic, self-centered entity that is generally unhappy with the world around it. The ego is childish and possessive and generally sees the world in terms of what is "mine" and what is "not mine".

What often happens in over half of all marriages is that after some time has passed, the married couple start to part ways energetically and spiritually, but because they made a Conscious Vow before God and their families, they feel a tremendous amount of guilt should the marriage ultimately fail. Even when couples manage to successfully divorce[7], the guilt and shame of breaking that vow continues to haunt them, which taints every subsequent relationship that follows to the point where happiness for either person is illusive.

Any of these lingering vows can be cleared on Chart 24, but in the same case as when we are clearing any blocking programs that are preventing us from setting the right intention in the

---

[7]   What is meant here by a "successful" divorce is that both couples manage to split their lives and their household congenially and are able to remain cordial, if not affectionate towards one another for the sake of their children, friends, extended families, etc.

first place, it is best to seek the help of a disinterested SRT practitioner whom you trust to do the clearing work. Divorces and separations can be extremely painful on an emotional and spiritual level, especially in cases where abuse or infidelity took place, so it is important that your healer can provide an outsider's perspective to help you clear those vows.

If after you have cleared all programs and blocks from the soul records and a couple still do not feel as though they belong together, then chances are that they need to live the rest of their lives apart. To discontinue a relationship can be an extremely emotional and difficult time for couples to endure, even when both parties believe that this is the best course of action. This becomes especially difficult when children are involved. However, we must remind ourselves that children selected their parents, which means that they came into this life knowing that they were not likely going to be together forever because there was a lesson in it that they needed to learn. Ultimately, the only souls we are completely responsible for is our own and if we sacrifice our own Spiritual health and development in order to perpetuate an illusion of happiness, then we are doing a disservice to ourselves and to the rest of our soul group.

So if you happen to be married or otherwise coupled with your soul partner, congratulations! You are in the minority. If you are ending a relationship and/or you want to keep looking for someone to share your soul journey with, do not despair. I hope the preceding paragraphs have given you a sound strategy for which you can set your intention to find the person you are looking for. Finally, if you wish to travel this path alone with nobody but SOURCE and your community of like-minded souls, that is wonderful, and I wish nothing but very best for you and your journey. May your friendships be strong and your chance encounters along your path be meaningful.

When evaluating your current relationship against your spiritual intention, you or a trusted SRT practitioner can use the following checklist based on what we learned in this chapter.

What was the percentage of Intention for Growth at the beginning of this relationship for each partner? • Partner #1: • Partner #2:	
What is the percentage of Intention for Growth currently for each partner? • Partner #1: • Partner #2:	
Is growth and/or Ascension in this relationship blocked?	
If yes: • From whom in the relationship is the block coming from? • Can we clear the blocking programs without research? • Please clear all blocking programs and ask the question again.	
If no: • Are there other programs on Chart 10a that are preventing this relationship from reaching its fullest potential? • Please clear all programs and blocks to Ascension and ask the question again.	
Are there any programs or blocks that are holding each other back from Ascension?	

If yes: • What is the percentage that my current partner is to assist me on my path to Ascension? • What is the percentage that my current partner is holding me back on my path to Ascension? • Please clear any programs and/or blocks and recheck percentages.	
If no: • Is this the best partnership I can be in for my own personal growth and journey to Ascension? • Is there another partnership that would be better for my personal growth and journey to Ascension?	

Chapter 5

Going Within

"Stillness is God." – Paramahansa Yogananda.

One of the first things you realize when you become an SRT Practitioner is that although the Work is transformational on an individual level, you need to share the Work in order to help bring about humanity's reconnection to SOURCE. In order to accomplish this, the Practitioner must attune themselves to being the conduit for High Self with minimal effort but maximum benefit for both themselves and for the people or clients they are working with.

This is why during the Basic and Advanced SRT classes, we spend so much of our time clearing ourselves and then practice clearing our fellow classmates. The idea is to elevate the soul of the student so that they may also become a clear channel for High Self. But although we spend a great deal of our efforts going through each of the treatment protocols to clear out blocking programs and negative emotions, programs have a tendency to re-assert themselves if we are not also doing the work to ensure that the old habits that created those programs in the first place are no longer repeated.

SPIRIT informs me that one of the major blocks to Refining our Consciousness to where we can become the conduit for High Self are "Additional Programs Type I and Type II at the ONE Level" (Chart 20). What I believe SPIRIT is trying to tell me is that we are constantly running programs that we tend to take for granted, but are inhibiting our ability to expand our consciousness to the point where energy work becomes automatic. These include our belief systems, our self-limiting ideas fed to us by our culture and poplar media, poor health, obsessive thinking, and our general inability to trust our inner vision and intuition.

Although Spiritual Response Therapy works on the level of SPIRIT, SRT is not a religion or a system of beliefs. Each SRT Practitioner brings to the table their own set of religious practices that enhance and deepen their understanding of how the Work is done. Where this can become a challenge is when a Practitioner's religious beliefs contradict the messages being received by High Self. High Self recognizes no individual soul to be superior to another. Yet, there are many faiths in the world that view practitioners of other faiths, no matter how similar that faith may be to their own, to be inferior even to the point where it is believed that followers of other faiths are evil, practicing a form of heresy or are otherwise damned by God.

Faiths that place one group of individual souls in a hierarchy above another group of souls have no place in SRT, as Universal SOURCE energy makes no such distinction. To hold such beliefs and be a Practitioner of SRT creates the negative block of "Conscious Control" (Chart 5) over the swing of the pendulum where the Practitioner's own belief system is controlling the outcome of the research, and not High Self.

"Blocked Chakras" (Chart 10a) can also affect the swing of the pendulum because if the body is not in harmony with its connection to the Earth, the Astral plane and Etheric plane, the practitioner's High Self and High Self Committee will have a more difficult time getting through.

We address the letting go of Conscious Control and unblocking Chakras in the Prep-to-Work phase of SRT. In addition to going through the motions of clearing both the physical and etheric bodies of all blocks and interferences, the SRT Practitioner should do all they can to seek a personal connection to High Self that goes beyond the use of the pendulum and the charts.

Working to become a consistent conduit of SOURCE energy in the work you do requires a level of commitment that you may not have realized when you first signed up for this. It requires silencing your conscious and subconscious mind of all the noise around you, and approaching the Work with a clear mind that is free of the assumptions and prejudices of the world. This is not easy as it requires that you "Believe" (Chart 19) that it can be done. Additionally, once you believe it, then you must take action on a regular basis in order to make it happen.

Living Outside of the Box

Our modern culture tries to convince us that in order to be happy, we must fill our schedules and our homes with as many activities and material stuff as possible. In addition to working a full-time job, which usually involves many hours of sitting in front of a computer or doing stressful and repetitive physical labor, we have a tendency to fill our "down time" with hobbies, clubs, sports teams, and politics. Some of us have more than one full-time job, or several part-time jobs in addition to our primary careers. If we have young children, add school activities, summer camps, and community service projects to the mix.

Most Americans do not get adequate rest or nutrition and so they wake up in the morning feeling tired and so they need to fill their bodies with caffeine and/or nicotine just to get moving. We take our meals at the drive thru, which we eat at our desks or in our cars. These meals generally consist of overly processed foods that are heavy in chemical-infused protein, fat, empty carbohydrates, sugar and salt. At night, we are so exhausted and stressed that we need to self-medicate with alcohol or prescription sleep aids just to wind ourselves down to the point where we can fall asleep.

Not only does such an unbalanced lifestyle eventually land you into an early grave, it fills our heads with self-limiting ideas that our lives begin and end with whatever is on our calendars and our social media accounts. Meanwhile, as our health continues to deteriorate, we start to base our self-worth on such superficial ideas like how many "likes" we get on Facebook, Twitter or Instagram. People who live this type of lifestyle find it nearly impossible to be a clear channel for SPIRIT energy. The ideal vessel for energy work is a person who is doing work that they love, but who also sets aside plenty of time in their day for rest, exercise, and meditation. Below are some simple tips to bring more order and balance into your life.

1) Do what you love, cut out the rest. Make a list of all the activities, chores, and hobbies that fill up your week and start to cut out those activities that you do not absolutely love to do. For the moment, forget about the things you feel you MUST do. If you do not LOVE doing it, cross it out.

2) Delegate the "must do's" you hate doing. If you do not
    love cutting your grass, hire a lawn service. If you hate
    cleaning your house, hire a cleaning service or get your
    family to pitch in more. Even some grocery stores are
    now providing personal shopping services where you
    simply give them your shopping list and they pick out
    all the groceries for you. Therefore, if you hate grocery
    shopping, you can now delegate that, too!

3) Take time for yourself. Schedule a regular time each day
    for self-care, but do your self-care in such a way that it
    does not add to the stress of your day. For example, if
    you like doing yoga but attending a class takes too much
    time out of your day, start practicing yoga at home.
    Go for regular walks outside whenever you can. If the
    weather is a limiting factor, use a treadmill, go to the
    gym or invest in some foul weather gear so you can still
    go outside even when the weather is bad. When you
    take your meals, take time to actually enjoy your food
    and fill it with healthy energy so that your body can
    receive the maximum benefit from it.

4) Cut out "mindless" entertainment. There is nothing
    wrong with taking a break for some entertainment, but
    only engage in entertainment that gives you joy and
    cut out all the rest. If watching the news or reading the
    newspaper adds to your stress, stop doing it. Bingeing
    on food is extremely unhealthy, so why is it acceptable
    to "binge" on an entire season of a television program
    over the course of a single weekend? Watching an
    occasional sports program might be entertaining, but is
    it healthy to spend your entire weekend, every weekend
    watching endless ball games?

5) Cut out unhealthy habits. Stop habitually taking substances that you know are not healthy for you, no matter how legal or socially acceptable they may be. Your daily cup(s) of coffee raises your blood pressure, depletes your adrenals, dehydrates your body, increases your mood swings and cuts your overall productivity. Tobacco causes a whole host of medical problems for both yourself, and the people in your household, including your pets. So if you smoke, stop. Drinking excess alcohol damages your liver, kills brain cells and impairs your brain's ability to function. So if you are the type of person who drinks until you are drunk, stop right now and promise yourself that you will never do it again.

6) Eat healthy foods. Eat only high vibration foods as demonstrated in Chapter 2, or if good choices are not available to you, energize your food so that it is healthier for your body as demonstrated in Chapter 3.

7) Surround yourself with healthy relationships. Build better relationships with the people you care about as demonstrated in Chapter 4.

You may look at the list above and think that some of the items are too difficult or impossible to take out of your life. Is it impossible, or are you too afraid to try? If you think there might be programs or blocks in the way, clear them. If resources or money is an issue, ask yourself if your current lifestyle or standard of living is where it is because you love it, or is it because of some ego-driven idea that does not bring you joy? If living beyond your means is causing you stress, downsize your lifestyle to the point where you have enough resources to do the things you love and none of the things that cause you stress.

A client of mine was complaining to me that he did not like the taste of water, so drinking six glasses of water a day was feeling like a chore to him. What I told him was that all he needed to do was to change his mind about the taste of the water. Is the water plain, or is it refreshingly clean? Is drinking water a chore, or is it a joy to cleanse the body of all the accumulated chemicals and waste? Is drinking water a conscious choice, or are you doing it because someone told you to? If cutting out an unhealthy habit feels like a chore, find joy in its opposite and it will be much easier to let the bad habits go.

In order to help others find balance in their own lives, we must first seek ways to find balance within ourselves. Clearing programs and blocks with SRT is a great place to start, but the real work comes when you reduce the noise in your life so that you can better be able to listen to what High Self is saying to you. At that point, you can then take that message from High Self and give it to others.

Meditation

One of the most effective ways to enhance your own ability to trust your inner vision and intuition is through a regular practice of meditation. Meditation will not only help you to quiet your mind from the bombardment of thoughts and emotions coming from your clients, it will help you quiet your mind from the noise of the world around you,

The world is full of many different ways to meditate. Some are better than others are. SPIRIT tells me that a good form of meditation is a practice that can take your soul back to where the concept of duality has not yet been introduced, and therefore the ego has nothing to cling onto to attempt to take control of you. You can do this by asking SPIRIT to indicate at what level on Chart 3 you need to connect and clear through meditation.[8] Getting to this level of soul consciousness through meditation alone can take a lifetime, but you can help the process along by asking High Self to provide you with the assistance you need.[9]

Beware of the trappings of so-called "commercial" meditation practices available on the market. The goal of meditation is to turn off your sensory inputs so that you can experience the silence of meditative bliss and connection to SOURCE. I have found that meditation music, videos, and chanting can actually add to the noise of the subconscious, making deep meditation impossible to achieve. Some practitioners who can achieve a meditative state while drumming, chanting, or playing music, but these practitioners were usually able to achieve those states of consciousness in silence before they learned to do so with the music.

The practice of yoga is a means to achieving a meditative state through movement, but you should practice yoga alone and in silence. A yoga class is an excellent way to learn how to do yoga, but too often, commercial yoga classes at a yoga studio tend to focus on physical fitness while downplaying the meditative movement and relaxation of a more authentic yogic experience. Therefore, if you wish to incorporate yoga into

[8] Robert indicates that even beings within the Spirit Realms on Chart 3 can be in discord due to the influence of the ego (Chart 32, Group 7, #1). This occurs because these illuminated beings are afraid of losing their personal identities if they become one with the ONE consciousness. If you should encounter this in your meditation practice, ask for the Angels of Light and High Council to work with these beings to release them from their fear and free them from ego.

[9] Please note, simply asking High Self to bring your soul consciousness to any level on Chart 3 does not get you out of meditating! It is meant solely as a means to provide assistance in your process and nothing more!

your meditative practice, learn how to do so without injury through a certified instructor, but then practice alone.

When meditating, close your eyes and the room you are in should be dark or nearly dark. Be sure that while you are meditating, that you eliminate as many things that will call your attention as possible. Turn off your telephone, close the door (with a "do not disturb" note on the doorknob if necessary), crate the dog, and turn off the computer and the television. Generally, the best time to medicate is between the hours of 5am and 6am and between 11pm and Midnight.[10] If you are worried that you will not get enough sleep by getting up so early and staying up so late, please note that people who meditate at least two hours a day generally require less sleep than people who do not meditate.

Before you begin, be sure to set your intention. You can do this by saying a short prayer or by simply asking High Self to help quiet your conscious and subconscious mind so that you may elevate your conscious mind to SOURCE. Whether you follow a prescribed meditative practice or whether you simply concentrate on your breathing until you reach a relaxed state is entirely up to your own comfort level. Some people choose to meditate while sitting on a cushion while others are comfortable sitting in a straight-backed chair. Do not meditate in a position that causes you a great deal of pain or discomfort as this will only distract you from relaxing your mind to the point where connection is possible. You should also avoid meditating while lying down or lounging on your bed unless there is a medical reason for you to do so. This is because if you are lying

---

[10]   On a vibrational level, these are good times to meditate, but on a practical level, these are the times of day when you are least likely to be disturbed because people are generally asleep at those times!

down, there is a risk that you will fall asleep. If you fall asleep, you are no longer meditating. You are sleeping.

If after you have tried your meditation practice and you find that you are not getting the results you are looking for, ask High Self if there are any programs you are running that are preventing you from meditating successfully, and clear them. Then try again.

If that does not work, then research different meditation practice methods until you and your High Self find one that works for you. Ideally, what you are looking for is a practice where you are in a near-sleep state but that your conscious mind is still awake to experience the connection to SOURCE energy. Cut off you sensory inputs such as touch, taste, smell, and hearing as if you are in a deep slumber, and silence the noise of your random subconscious thoughts, memories, and problem solving.

Some days will be easier than others. There will be days where you will be unsuccessful at shutting out the noises of the outside world from banging around in your head, and there will be other days where finding the silence will feel effortless. The point is to keep practicing no matter what life throws at you, and remembering that just because you were able to meditate successfully one day, does not mean you will be able to do it every day. Eventually, after years of consistent practice, meditation will come as naturally to you as breathing!

The practice of reordering your life to be more conducive to being a conduit for High Self is the best way to enable yourself to be the beacon that will attract people to you that you can help through SRT. Our world will try to make this difficult for you by bombarding you with ideas, products and images promising to make this process easy, but the process of simplification, love and connection is a deeply personal one that cannot be acquired, purchased or sold.

Chapter 6

Finding Your Personal Power

The primary goal of all SRT sessions is for the Practitioner to assist the client in finding their own personal power, but how does the Practitioner find that power within them? As we have seen in the preceding chapters, we can ask High Self to help us make good choices and help us change our lives for the better, but can we ask High Self to light the spark of power within ourselves? If so, how do we do that? SPIRIT has presented us with the gift of SRT, and as such "we are the Healers of All" (Chart 26). However, in order to help heal the world, we need to be sure that we have healed ourselves so that we can bring this gift to others.

Ascension is the ultimate destiny for all of humanity. That "thought" (Chart 13) was planted into the collective unconscious before we were even created. As an SRT Practitioner, you are part of an army of light warriors who are now helping to make that destiny a reality, one person at a time. All it takes is "faith" and "desire" to become part of that process, and an unconditional "love" for all of humanity to see this to the end (Chart 19).

It all begins with the conscious decision to heal ourselves. In this instance, we are not just talking about making good choices and reducing our stress, but we are also talking about staying healthy both mentally and physically. We all have programs we need to have cleared, and we all have programs that will only show themselves once other programs are clear. Therefore, the act of clearing is a never-ending process of discovery and growth.

About 15 years ago, I received a diagnosis of Hashimoto's thyroiditis. Hashimoto's thyroiditis is an autoimmune disease in which your own body gradually destroys your thyroid gland. Nobody knows what causes this disease, but what we do know is that most patients who have this condition experience hypothyroidism, which comes with symptoms such as weight gain, chronic fatigue, constipation, depression and generalized pain. After several years, the prognosis is that patients will eventually develop complications such as thyroid lymphoma (a type of thyroid cancer), but most commonly, the thyroid eventually shrinks to the point where it is no longer producing enough hormone to regulate the autonomic functions of the body. This can lead to even greater complications since the thyroid gland is essentially the "captain" of your body's automatic functions such as blood pressure, metabolism, and digestion.

At the time of my diagnosis, I had already starting developing some of the symptoms of hypothyroidism, which is what prompted my doctor to order the blood test to confirm what he suspected. The typical treatment for Hashimoto's is with levothyroxine, a synthetic thyroid hormone designed to treat the symptoms of hypothyroidism without really addressing the disease itself, since the "cause" of Hashimoto's is generally unknown. The problem with the medication is that by replacing your body's thyroid hormone artificially, it may actually accelerate the condition to the point where the thyroid gland stops producing natural hormone on its own long before the disease takes its course. After receiving the diagnosis, I made a conscious decision to reverse this condition on my own using natural means. Losing my thyroid gland and being dependent on an artificial hormone for the rest of my life was simply unacceptable.

SPIRIT informs me that "Conscious Mind Programs Type I" (Chart 14) are often caused by "Programs the Soul is Unaware of" (Chart 11) (i.e. programs in the Subconscious and Unconscious minds). What this typically does is it blocks the conscious mind from being the "Inquirer" (Chart 8a) for out-of-the-box solutions, and that ignorance eventually leads to a "Fall from Grace" (Chart 16) (i.e. chronic or terminal disease).

Think of your conscious mind like the captain of a ship at sea standing on the bridge giving out orders. While the captain is the one who is in command of the ship, it is the crew's responsibility to carry out the captain's orders. If the crew lacks the proper training to do their jobs, and/or they lack the resources to receive the necessary training, then it makes no difference how many times the captain repeats their orders, the ship will be going nowhere.

The metaphor of the Captain of the ship is especially appropriate given that the Conscious Mind's primary purpose is to be the communicator to both the inside and the outside world. The Subconscious Mind (the crew) is not only the holder of recent memories; it also gathers the necessary resources from the Unconscious Mind in order to help the Conscious Mind do what it wants to do. The Unconscious Mind is the storehouse of memories, even those that the Conscious Mind intentionally wants to forget. In addition, the Unconscious Mind holds your core beliefs, habits, and behaviors.

When you make the conscious decision to change something important in your life, the first step is to be absolutely committed to changing the condition or behavior you want to change. Then you need to train both your Subconscious and your Unconscious minds to carry out your orders. This will require you to use SRT to clear the Subconscious and Unconscious programs that are already in place, and to replace them with new programs and beliefs that support your Conscious decision.

For example, when I decided that my thyroid was going to remain whole and functional for the rest of my life, I then needed to convince my Subconscious and Unconscious mind that is was not only possible, but it was going to happen. The first thing I needed to do was to clear all of the unconscious beliefs and programs that allowed me to surrender my personal power to the idea that there was nothing I could do to change my condition except simply managing my symptoms. Once those programs were clear, I then replaced them with the belief that alternative treatment strategies would be effective at reversing the condition to the point where all indications where it even existed would be gone. This did not happen overnight. It involved finding a new doctor who supported my conscious decision, gaining the support and belief from my family that I could do this, and I also needed to change several habits and beliefs in order to support my new paradigm.

I am pleased to report that in my last blood test there was no indication that I ever had Hashimoto's disease. A skeptic may say that the original diagnosis must have been mistaken, and a person of faith may say that a "miracle" occurred, but they would both be wrong.[11] What had actually happened was

---

[11] See Chapter 14.

that my conscious choice to be free of this disease, coupled with the re-training of my "crew", changed the reality of my physical condition to the point where it simply did not exist at any point in space or time.

In addition to making the conscious choice to take back your personal power, there are strategies you can employ with every encounter with the people in your life that will strengthen your sense of self and prevent you from giving away your power to others. These include, Lowering your Energetic Shields, opening yourself to Doing the Work on a daily basis, and to commit yourself to constant self-education and personal growth.

Lowering your Energetic Shields

While I was living in New Mexico, Nina and I attended to a workshop consisting of acupuncturists, Reiki healers, and other energy practitioners. The purpose of the workshop was to learn how to protect ourselves from the negative energies of their clients. Over three days, we learned how to create an energetic barrier around the Chakra located at the solar plexus, and we learned strategies about how we can detach ourselves from empathy for our clients. The idea was that if the practitioner could emotionally divest themselves from their client, then they would be able to do the work without losing their own personal power in the process.

The concern that these energy workers had was that when they work with clients who are unable to generate their own personal power, their client will attempt to steal their power either consciously or unconsciously if the practitioner does nothing to protect himself or herself. After leaving the workshop, we tried to practice the techniques we learned, but something about cutting ourselves off from the energy of our clients seemed contrary to being healers.

SPIRIT informs me that energy practitioners who deploy shields while they work are running "Body Programs" (Chart 10b) where due to some past life trauma or psychic wound; they feel they need to protect their bodies from the very people they are trying to help. This does not work, and if you are running such a program, you should work to clear it.

When your High Self is consistently operating at the consciousness levels at RADIANT LOVE and above on Chart 3, you have tapped into the most abundant source of energy imaginable! Energy from SOURCE is made of pure light and pure love and never runs out. Only the ego can stop the flow of energy from SOURCE. The ego believes that some people are "good" and some people are "bad" and that we need to open ourselves up to the good people and protect ourselves from the bad people. SOURCE energy recognizes no soul to be good or bad, and if a person is drawn to you to seek your help, why would you want to cut yourself off to them when their soul is no different from your own?

We are not perfect people. When we research our own past lives, we find several where we have done horrible things to other souls. Does that knowledge make us less deserving of love and compassion? Of course not! Do those horrible things we did in our past lives not matter because they happened in another life? Again, no, of course it matters because we carry the things we do to others from one lifetime to the next.

Time exists at a single point in all realities and all dimensions, so the sins we committed in our past lives are just as fresh and just as present as if we committed them yesterday. In fact, those of us who are called to be healers in this lifetime were most often the most horrible, evil people you can possibly imagine in other lifetimes! If we can forgive those unredeemable souls because we are all worthy of redemption and healing, so it must also be true for those souls who committed their sins or who are otherwise suffering in this lifetime and who need our help now.

Therefore, our conclusion with regard to the employment of energetic shields is that as long as the practitioner has a strong connection with High Self and they can see all souls as worthy of redemption and healing, then there is no need to be fearful that anyone will take away your power from you.[12] Will some clients attempt to drain you of your power? Yes, they will. However, the choice to allow your client to drain your energy or to tap into the endless energy reserves of the Universe is entirely up to you.

Doing the Work on a Daily Basis

Another way to build your personal power is by doing the work whenever you can, as often as you can. Even if you have nobody to work on now, the world is always full of souls in need of clearing. "World Energies (Positive and Negative)" (Chart 5) are constantly challenging humanity to think in dualistic, ego-driven terms, but as mankind moves closer to ascension, a kind of cognitive dissonance is occurring where people know that the world is an illusion, but at the same time they feel compelled to participate in it no matter how much it hurts them. These souls are reaching out to anyone who can help them, even if they do not know from whence that help is coming from. Perhaps their request for help is in a form of

---

[12]   The "Triple Shield" that we use in the prep to work is to trap and remove disincarnates as we do our work. Do not use the Triple Shield to block yourself from your own clients.

a prayer, or perhaps their High Self Committee is sending out an S.O.S. to anyone who can help.[13]

Whenever you can find the time, make it a point to spend about an hour or two a week to sit down with your charts to help souls in need. I like to think of it as God's answering service, where I open up the cosmic hotline to help people in need. People pray every day, but they rarely expect to hear an answer. Because SRT transcends space, time and distance, you can be that answer for someone today.

One of my hobbies is that I like to make and collect pendulums, which I sell at events I attend. What I like to do is I grab a handful and put them on the table in front of me. I then ask SPIRIT to guide any souls who need clearing to each of the pendulums on the table, and I give a clearing to each one until the table is empty.

Some days I ask SPIRIT to provide me with only those souls who need past life clearings. Other days I ask SPIRIT to provide me with souls who need Spirit Programs cleared. Most days I simply ask SPIRIT to give me whoever needs clearing. If I am starting to feel out of practice with a particular type of protocol such as an Inner Child Progression or Brain Restructuring, I will ask SPIRIT to provide me with only those souls who need those types of clearings. Since each soul is different, each mini-session follows the same protocols that we provide to any client who sees me. Each receives a prep to work, a clearing, and a mop-up. I generally limit it to one clearing per pendulum so that I can clear as many different souls I can.

---

[13] Robert used to ask SPIRIT give him someone in the local hospital to work on. In the SRT Dictionary, he suggests helping folks who may be attempting or thinking of committing suicide within a specific mile radius.

This practice of providing random clearings will benefit you in two ways. At the surface level, what you will be doing is helping to make a real difference for not only the souls you are reaching, but you will be providing help for all of humanity. For each prayer you answer, you are helping to make the world a better place for everyone the "client" and everyone for whom that client is close to. As we help others reduce the influence of the ego, the more people will come to realize that we are ALL ONE, and perhaps more people will learn how to love more, and hate less. True, this will not happen overnight, but if each SRT Practitioner in the world does this at least once a week, think of the hundreds of thousands of people we will influence!

On the second level, doing this work trains your soul to be the compassionate conduit for SPIRIT energy that you need to be. You will increase your personal power with each clearing you do as you build your confidence in each of the protocols. By working on "anonymous" souls remotely, you are completely free to clear those souls absent of any prejudices you might have had if that person was sitting in front of you.

Very quickly, you learn that the best way to be the channel for High Self is to be free and open to the love of SOURCE so that the next time a client sits down with you, all you will see is their beautiful soul and not the ego-driven mess you might have judged them to be before.

Commit Yourself to a Journey of Self-Discovery

While the focus of this book is SRT and most of what we have spoken about in this book is about SRT, there is a lot more to life than SRT! Not all problems in life can be resolved with SRT. If you are feeling stuck with a program you cannot seem to clear using the pendulum, there is no harm is seeking another healing modality to get the job done. In the following chapter, we will discuss how you can build your healing community with a variety of different healers and disciplines.

The journey of self-discovery is a quest that always has a beginning, but never has an end. For each question the Universe answers, a hundred more questions take its place and each one seems to take us even closer to God. During the 18th and 19th Centuries in the Age of Enlightenment, science made a deliberate effort to divorce God from Nature. However, starting in the late 20th Century and continuing on into the 21st Century, each new scientific discovery is taking us back to God as we start to understand that the fabric of the Universe is as much about the mind and matter itself is merely the illusion!

There are literally thousands of energetic healing modalities in the world today, each with its own protocols and systems of belief. Even among SRT Practitioners, each person brings their own system of beliefs and training into how they connect and facilitate healing through SRT. The important thing to remember is that all healing practices, provided they be connected to SOURCE and not the ego, each bring with it their own special blend of wisdom that can benefit both you and your clients. You can literally spend a lifetime learning as many healing practices as you can and you would not even scratch the surface of all the wisdom that is available to you!

Chapter 7

Building Your Healing Community

Human beings are social creatures so we need to build communities. While there are some of us who are perfectly happy to live alone on a mountaintop, the majority of humanity tends to gather into tribes of like-minded individuals in order to build groups that mutually benefit each other. The size of these communities depends largely on your personal comfort level and your individual needs. While some prefer the crowded and somewhat impersonal nature of large cities, others prefer a suburban environment where neighbors are on a first name basis and where children tend to go to the same schools. My 10 year-old son prefers his community to be via the Internet where he can experience a rich tapestry of cultures and experiences not limited by language or geography.

Your healing community is no different. Whether you prefer a healing community of hundreds or a community of only one or two trusted friends, depends largely on your individual tastes and needs. You may be wondering whether you even need a healing community at all, but consider this.

As an SRT Practitioner, your first responsibility is to your own self-care, and while there is a lot you can do yourself with SRT, it is often very difficult to self-diagnose and self-clear something your own ego does not want you to see. Even if your healing community consists of only one other healer, they will be able to see things in you that you cannot, and vice versa.

It is important to recognize that the members of your healing community are all operating from the "New Paradigm" above RADIANT LOVE on Chart 3, no matter what their primary healing modality happens to be. This is not to say that they must also be SRT Practitioners. On the contrary, what you want is a diverse group of individuals who approach healing from their own point of view. Another important characteristic for the members of your healing community is a strong degree of trust and a promise that no matter what, you will speak the truth to each other, no matter how much it may hurt the ego of the other.[14]

My wife and I are our own mini-healing community, but we also have other healers within our circle of friends and professional associations either with whom we provide a trade for service or to whom we maintain a strictly professional relationship. Currently, our personal healing community consists of a Medical Doctor who also practices holistic medicine, a Chiropractor, two massage therapists, a tarot card reader, and a yoga instructor. Our extended healing community consists of my SRT Teacher, other members of the Spiritual Response Association (SRA), our Dentist, and the Vermont Acupuncture Council. On top of that, we add the various current and former

---

[14] While it is always important to "speak truth" whenever working with clients or members of your community, it is also important that you do so with compassion and love. When egos are hurt, they tend to speak louder than compassion!

clients who have access to knowledge and resources to help us keep healthy and active. We also have several friends who are willing to offer themselves as guinea pigs whenever we are working on developing new treatment protocols or we need practice new techniques we just learned, and vice versa.

Building your healing community occurs in much the same way as finding the right partner as we discussed in Chapter 4. Except in this instance, instead of simply putting it out in the Universe that "Intension is Growth", SPIRIT informs me that "Experience is the Process" (Chart 27), which is to mean that soul experience is gained through the collaboration of like-minded souls who may have different paths but similar goals.

Drawing together your personal healing community should be an organic process that begins with increasing one's "Awareness" of their own personal health needs, and to "Draw in Energy" to attract the right practitioners who not only have the skills you need, but who can also benefit from the skills that you have as a healer (Chart 19). Once you have the right combination of healers in your circle of friends and associations, a "Solidified Pattern" (Chart 24) of give and take is established where everyone gets exactly what they need at the time they need it, and a satisfactory exchange of energy takes place.

As time goes on, do not be surprised as your healing community evolves with some practitioners leaving and new practitioners coming in. If the intention from everyone remains solid, and all parties continue to be operating from the maximum vibration, your circle will evolve as everyone's individual needs change over time.

One of the challenges with maintaining a healing community, no matter how large or small, is making sure that everyone remains working at the maximum vibration, and that nobody's ego starts to assert itself above the others.

There is always a temptation for healers to place themselves on some sort of hierarchy where some healing modalities are valued more than others. For example, a Practitioner who received their primary education by obtaining an advanced college or university degree or they had to go through some form of internship, residency or formal licensing process may place themselves in higher regard than a Practitioner who is self-taught or received their training outside of the mainstream educational system. Likewise, some healing practitioners may hold certain prejudices or exclusive religious opinions directed at certain healing modalities that they view as invalid in some way.

SPIRIT recognizes all such hierarchies as inventions of the ego and dualistic space, so no one in your healing community who believes in such archaic distinctions is operating at New Paradigm above RADIANT LOVE. You can work to raise a person's vibration by clearing any programs that might be getting in the way, but if they insist on holding onto those beliefs, their energy is only bringing down the collective vibration of the group and so they should be encouraged to seek a different community elsewhere.

Another challenge with healing communities occurs on occasions when healers are exchanging their services in lieu of collecting a fee. The reason why we collect a fee for our services is not only to allow us the ability to buy the things we need to survive and thrive, but also the exchange of money is a form of energetic exchange. In this exchange, the client expresses their acceptance and gratitude of the energy you are giving in the form of money. The challenge comes in when one of the members of your healing group is providing services to the others, but the others are not reciprocating the energetic exchange for whatever reason. This creates an imbalance of energy between the practitioners, which can lower the vibration of the relationship to the point where one party starts to feel as though the other is taking advantage of them.

The best way to avoid such misunderstandings is to establish a monetary value of the services each of you are providing so that when services are exchanged, a like-kind exchange can take place where there are no misunderstandings. Another good idea is to make the trade in services within a specified period or to provide the other with a coupon, gift certificate or some other form of written I.O.U. I would encourage you to avoid "running a tab" or making like-kind exchanges with practitioners who lack the ability to return a service of equal value.

There was a time where I once traded SRT services with one such practitioner. At first, the exchange worked out just fine where I would perform the service and within a month, I would get a like-kind service in exchange. After seeing good results with the services I provided, the practitioner also wanted me to do the same exchange for other members of their family, each time increasing the number of services owed back to me for each additional person in their family I serviced. Within a short period, this practitioner owed me a lot more services than I could possibly use. So rather than continuing to create a further imbalance in in the relationship, I decided to end the exchange and insist on charging my normal fee. In the interest of our friendship, I did not insist on receiving payment for the services already rendered, but I had to make it clear that the energetic exchange was too unbalanced to continue. The practitioner promised to "pay off their tab" before continuing with any more sessions with me, but unfortunately, I never heard from them again.

Was this person simply trying to take advantage of me? I honestly believe that was not their original intent, but as time went on and the exchange became more unbalanced, I have to wonder. Today I avoid such misunderstanding by completing our like-kind exchanges within one month of when we did the original service. Another option is to avoid like-kind exchanges altogether and simply charge my normal fee whether I are seeing people within my personal healing community or not.

If you have no plans on doing SRT professionally and you believe you will only be performing clearings for friends and family, that does not mean you should ignore the cautionary tale above. Just because you do not charge money for your services, does not mean you should simply give away your services to anyone.

As we all know, what we do as SRT Practitioners has the ability to change people on a very deep and spiritual level, and so there needs to be some sort of energetic exchange between you and whomever you work for, otherwise you will be creating an energetic imbalance. Energetic exchanges do not need to be "healing" in nature for the exchange to be legitimate. Exchanges for babysitting services, vegetables from the garden, dinner at a restaurant or even just to take time for a friendly phone call may be enough. We measure the legitimacy of the exchange by the amount of gratitude we express to one another after the work is finished. As long as the giver has no expectation of reward, and the receiver is under no obligation to give it, but all parties express gratitude for the experience, then all is well and nobody owes anyone anything.

Your SRT Community

Now I would like to spend some time telling you about your official SRT Community. As an SRT Practitioner, you are part of a network of healers that spans the entire globe! Throughout the 1990's and early 2000's, Robert Detzler crossed the world to bring the gift of SRT to as many people as he could find. During that time, he helped to found the Spiritual Response Association (SRA), which is currently located in the Pacific Northwest of the United States near Seattle, Washington. With a small paid staff and an army of volunteers, the purpose of the SRA has always been to help bring this healing modality to as many people as possible.

Even though Robert is no longer with us physically, his legacy lives on within the thousands of students he taught. Our continued connection to High Self through this system we call SRT is a testament to his life and work. The connection lives on, our understanding continues to deepen, and humanity's path to ascension continues on its steady course.

After completing your first Basic class, you will automatically receive the monthly news magazine *Ascension* to either your email or mailbox. In it you will find the latest news in the world of SRT as well as a list of classes you can take to further your journey into this healing modality. Even if you have no plans on becoming a Certified Consultant or Teacher, I strongly urge you to maintain your subscription to *Ascension* after your trial subscription runs out. I would also urge you to consider being a sustaining donor to the organization so that they can continue the good work they are doing to bring the gift of SRT to the world.

If you ever need to speak to a fellow SRT Practitioner or Teacher, they are only a few clicks away whether your fellow

Practitioners live in the next town or the next country. The SRA keeps a list of all current Consultants, Teachers and staff at the SRA on their website along with their contact information. Each one of them is always happy to provide you with any help and support you need whether you need a full clearing, or if you simply have questions you need answered.

Naturally, your first line of support in the SRT Community will always be your SRT Teacher. Whether you are a Basic Practitioner or a Certified Consultant, your teacher is your primary resource and gateway into the world of SRT. They were there for you as you started to learn how to navigate the charts, they continue to be your sounding board for when things seem confusing to you. If your original SRT teacher is no longer available, feel free to reach out to any others on the SRA website.

Your next level of your SRT Community consists of your fellow students. Whether you received your Basic and/ or Advanced training in a class with twelve other students or whether you participated in a class of only one, your SRT teacher can help get you in touch with other people who are on the same level of understanding you are. Your classmates are excellent for bouncing off ideas or for simply practicing the various techniques and protocols. Several SRT teachers hold monthly conference calls where former students are welcome to gather to discuss ideas or to reinforce knowledge of the charts and concepts from your class. There are also several Social Media pages specifically set up for SRT Practitioners that are not open to the general public where Practitioners are free to discuss ideas and challenges they might be facing.

Whether you choose to further your SRT education and become a Certified Consultant or whether you decide to integrate SRT into whatever healing modality you happen to

PART II

TAKING YOUR GIFT TO THE WORLD

Chapter 8

Hanging Up Your Shingle

My wife, Nina, and I run a joint healing venture called "Vital Bioenergetics" (ninagee.com). I am a Certified SRT Consultant and Nina is a licensed Acupuncturist who practices a form of Esoteric Acupuncture that incorporates vibrational medicine, sacred geometry, chakra cleansing, shamanic healing, and a smattering of nutrition, herbal and crystal healing techniques.

While I was working my way up in the corporate world, Nina was the sole proprietor of two Acupuncture practices, one in Pennsylvania and another in New Jersey. Like millions of other people around the world, the financial crash of 2008 was not kind to us. For eight years, we needed to change addresses several times, as we worked to put our lives back together. A job opportunity for me landed us in Vermont, and once we decided that Vermont was a place we wanted to settle, Nina decided to re-open her practice.

It had been eight years since Nina saw anyone professionally as an acupuncturist, so when we decided to give it a trial run, we decided to try opening a community clinic in downtown Rutland at the Pyramid Holistic Healing Center, Rutland's only esoteric healing center and rock shop. In addition to selling rocks and semiprecious gems, the location also hosted yoga classes, massage therapy, a salt cave, tarot readings, and dance and fitness programs. For five months, Nina ran her community clinic three nights a week on the second floor of the Pyramid where she saw walk-in clients whom she charged only $15 per session.

After limited success and a change in ownership at the Pyramid, Nina accepted an offer to open a more traditional acupuncture practice at a chiropractor's office where she would see clients three days a week.

I had been an SRT Practitioner since 2003, but up until we moved to Vermont, I would only do clearings for friends and family. After doing some clearings for some friends we met at the Pyramid, I was encouraged to consider doing SRT professionally, and after consulting with High Self on the subject, I began the process of obtaining my Consultant Certification through the Spiritual Response Association.

It was at this point that Nina felt that she and I should combine our skills so that we could eventually create a fully integrated practice together. The concept behind our practice is that it would be a place where clients could not only receive healing and relief from their pain and other physical symptoms, but that they would also receive spiritual life coaching to they can move on from their physical and emotional problems and start to live their best lives! After consulting with High Self again, we formed Vital Bioenergetics. We immediately started treating clients at our home where we combined SRT Clearings, Esoteric Acupuncture, and other forms of vibrational medicine.

At the time of this writing, our business currently works out of two locations. The first location is our home in Vermont, and the second is in two rented rooms at the chiropractor's office. As with most businesses at this stage of development, our cash flow goes through periods of feast and famine. Some months we are seeing several clients every week, and some months we see only a few.

The point of the above story is to illustrate that your healing practice, no matter what it looks like when you first "hang up your shingle" and open your doors to clients, it is going to evolve and change over time. We had no idea that the little pop-up community clinic we established in downtown Rutland would evolve into a growing energetic healing practice with clients from all over the world two years later?

If you and SPIRIT believe you should turn your SRT skills into a business, how you begin that journey will be largely dependent on the types of resources you have at your disposal and who else you know within your own healing community. You may start out as a part-time venture in a shared practice, you may start out in a small booth at a psychic faire or if you have the resources, you may be able to rent your own downtown office space complete with all of the branding and marketing support you could ask for. No matter how humble your beginnings, if you remain true to yourself and to your personal healing style, SPIRIT assures me that you will be successful!

In the next three chapters, SPIRIT and I will do our best to provide you with tips and advice on how to open and maintain your healing practice, especially in those precarious first few years of operation, which is where the majority of new businesses fail. However, unlike other start-up businesses, a healing practice where you are continually connected to High Self and you are doing the work of assisting others in their own ascension, has a much better chance at being successful than businesses that are not connected to High Self. The choice of whether your business succeeds or fails (and "choice" is the right word), is up to you to make because all the help you can possibly want to help you succeed is waiting for you to simply ask for it.

Choice

As beings with free will, we can choose which path in life we wish to take. SPIRIT can provide us with the guidance and SPIRIT can clear our path of the soul programs that hinder our ascension along that path, but it is our decision as to whether we choose to walk that path or whether we choose to take a different one. With the benefit of hindsight, after we have spent our considerable time and resources arriving at this point, where we must make a choice, we suddenly realize that the choice in front of us is really no choice at all. If it is within our path to bring the gift of healing and ascension to the world, then it is likely that we chose this path before we were even born, whether we were fully aware of it or not.

Any other choice you make, whether it is to stay at the job with the nice 401K or whether it is to stay at home to be the happy homemaker, those choices are likely guided by the ego, and not by High Self. As we have said before, the ego is the selfish, apathetic and generally unhappy entity that connects your physical body to the dualistic ideas of right and wrong, good and bad, and scarcity and abundance. The ego wants to be lazy. The ego wants to play it safe. The ego could care less about humanity's journey to ascension because the ego knows how hard that can be, and the ego does not like things to be hard. When toddlers start to act out because their caregiver is telling them to do something they do not want to do, we send them into a quiet corner for a "time out" so they can calm down and accept whatever is being asked of them. Therefore, if you are starting to feel your ego go into a temper tantrum because you want to do something it thinks is risky, your first step on this journey is to tell your ego to take a "time out" while you figure out what your next move should be.

Your ego will tell you that choosing the path of the healer will make you poor, but this is generally not the case at all. SPIRIT will never ask you to forsake all of your worldly possessions and live out your days begging on the streets in your bare feet. SPIRIT wants you to do the work to help humanity, and how can you do that if you are homeless?

What SPIRIT will be asking you to do is to reshape your life in such a way that you continually bring the gift of healing to the world and to throw away all of the things that feed the ego and brings unhappiness and scarcity into your life. If done right, and if you stay connected to High Self, not only will you be able to meet your physical and financial needs, while doing the work you love, but you will be living a life that is more in line with your connection to SPIRIT.

Choosing your Business Model

How you shape your new business is as personal and unique as you are. Just because the typical healing practice may consist of professional office, a website, and a treatment room does not mean that you need to follow suit. The key is to take a close look at your professional background up to this point in your life, and play on your strengths while working to build something as completely different and unique as you are. Remember that everything in your life has been leading you to this point and this moment. Do not discount any skill, experience, or association you have built up over your lifetime. Your skills and experience will make your practice as unique and special as you are!

Nina has a background in acupuncture and esoteric research, but she also has skills as an award-winning artist, event planner, marketing director and graphic designer. I have a background in teaching, financial planning and accounting, business administration, contracts, event planning and writing.

Therefore, we not only have a business where we can minimize administrative overhead costs, we know we attract clients who are fellow entrepreneurs who need help clearing energetic blocks to running their businesses. Nina has spent a great deal of her life overcoming many challenging physical and emotional conditions where Western medicine was unable to provide any help, so her clients tend to be people who are diagnosed with challenging chronic conditions where hope of any sort of recovery is in short supply.

We both have a background in education, music and art, so we have incorporated those things into what we offer our clients. Therefore, we are building a retreat curriculum, we are both starting to learn Kirtan, and both Nina and I are working towards a teaching certification (myself in SRT, and Shamanic healing for Nina). Eventually, we envision our home being a healing retreat and learning space where we incorporate education, music and art to create a holistic healing experience unlike anything our future clients have ever experienced before.

Whether Vital Bioenergetics evolves into what we envision in the future is not really the point because as time goes by, we are going to evolve and change and so will our healing practice. The point is that even though most healing practices tend to start the same way, how they evolve over time has everything to do with the individual journey of the practitioner who directs it.

Lee Harris (leeharrisenergy.com) has a background in music and performance. In 2004, he started doing part-time intuitive readings out of his home in England. Like most energy sensitives, he did not ask for this ability to channel higher wisdom, but once he realized that he had no choice but to share his gift with others, his path became clearer to him. His background in music and performance helped to make him a natural public speaker, and his knowledge of media marketing allowed his messages to reach a wider audience. Today, Lee is the owner of a multi-media, worldwide event company and production house. He provides individual healing sessions and business coaching for other energy healers as well as hosting large scale seminars that attract thousands of followers and participants.

Dr. Karen Kan (karenkan.com) has a background as a medical doctor, life coach and teacher. Before becoming an energetic healer, she was an instructor at the UCLA Medical School where she was an engaging presenter as well as an excellent advisor for her students. After moving to Lake Placid with her husband and suffering from a life-threatening illness, she decided to leave her medical career behind so she could pursue an alternative healing practice. Her current practice that focuses on one-on-one life coaching designed to train people to become "light warriors", while also treating clients suffering from chronic pain by connecting them to Universal Light Energy. Her presentation background skills allows her to produce her own YouTube channel, Internet radio show, and organizes "Light Warrior" retreats and training programs all out of her home in upstate, New York.

Walt Thiessen (loatoday.net) has a background in social media, web design, and broadcasting. For several years, he ran a political discussion forum and an Internet radio talk show on alternative media that focused on economics and politics. After his own spiritual awakening involving the "Law of Attraction", he gave up his political talk show and replaced it with a show that focuses on spirituality and attracting wealth and happiness called "Law of Attraction Today". The daily radio show has listeners from all over the world as Walt and life-coaches trained in the Law of Attraction discuss ways their listeners can bring physical and spiritual abundance into their lives.

As you can see, there is no typical alternative healing practice model out there as each practice is as unique as the person who runs it. In order for your own practice to bring you both joy and abundance, it needs to both play to your strengths as a healer and your strengths from wherever you came from. Your whole life has been preparing you for the moment you decided to become an alternative healer. Build on the strength of the skills you have accumulated in your lifetime as you build new skills and allow abundance to enter your life!

Clear All Blocks

Starting your own business is a very daunting task. It is a common statistic that 95% of all new businesses fail within their first five years of operation, and that even if the business is a success, it generally will not be profitable until the second or third year of operations. There are literally hundreds of rational reasons why we should go back to our cubicles and our "safe" jobs rather than venturing out to become an energy healing entrepreneur.

Therefore, your first step should always be to take out the pendulum and after you have completed the Prep to Work and reduced the ego to less than 3%, and start clearing all the blocks that are preventing you from moving forward with your venture. If your responses from the pendulum do not feel right or are inconsistent, it may be that your ego is pushing through despite your best efforts to keep it at bay. Check to see to what degree the ego is influencing the pendulum. If you get a response greater than 10%, then you should find someone else to be the conduit for High Self for you.

When making any kind of big decision in your life, whether it is starting a new business or something more personal, it can be very difficult for you to let go of the results to the point where your ego does not influence the swing of the pendulum. Whoever you pick to throw the pendulum for you should have no stake in the success or failure in whatever it is you are asking and you should be able to receive an accurate response.[15]

Getting Started

This is the scariest part of all, and if you can get past this initial point, you should be all right. Once you decide to get started, you learn very quickly about what you do not know as opposed to what you actually know. While it is important to have a clear plan when you first start out, you also need to stay open to the idea that this thing is going to evolve and change very quickly once things get moving.

Whether you have thousands of dollars to get started or whether you only have a pocket full of dreams, you are going to need help getting your venture off the ground. If you have limited resources and skills but you have people who believe in you, do not be shy about asking for their expertise and their help. You will be surprised at what types of skills certain friends or family members are willing to give. If someone is willing

---

[15]   See Chapter 2.

to give you some help and/or basic training in exchange for an SRT clearing, learn how to say yes, and thank you.[16]

You may want to start out by joining a co-op or collective practice with other healers. The biggest advantage with joining an established practice is that you can sometimes benefit from referrals from the other practitioners. Another advantage is that you may have professional help available to you as part of your rent in the form of a receptionist or office manager. There may already be a group website and/or other marketing materials already built into the practice, and you may have an office available to give your beginning practice a well-established and professional look.

The potential downside to joining a group practice is that rents tend to be expensive (depending on the location), there is a risk you may become a voice in a chorus to potential clients rather than the shining beacon you want to be. Another possibility is that you may not get along with your fellow healers. If you are considering joining a group practice, check with High Self to see if your personality will mix well with the other practitioners in the office, and then give it a trial run for a few months to see how things work out. You may even discover that working at a group practice is where you are naturally happiest, where your fellow practitioners are not only your roommates, but they are also your best friends. One day you may discover that your individual practice is outgrowing the group practice and at that point, you will need to find your own space or start your own group practice somewhere else.

---

[16]   If you are concerned that a friend or family member's skills in a particular area may not be exactly what you need, be sure to check in with High Self and ask that only the people who will provide you with the maximum benefit to your venture be guided to help you.

Whatever you do, when you do it, make the work look and feel like this is exactly what you want to be doing at the time you are doing it. SPIRIT informs me that the best advice is to "Act as If" (Chart 19) when you are at this beginning stage. If you are only seeing one client a week, "act as if" you are seeing however many clients you think you should be seeing by doing clearings on random souls who need it.[17] Soon you will be seeing more clients because you have informed the Universe that you are now open for business and High Self will start bringing the souls to you who need your help.

The last thing you should always keep in mind no matter how your practice is going, is that it is likely going to change and evolve over time. Whether you start out as a solo practitioner working psychic fairs or a member of a group practice, be open to where the next step will lead you. High Self will be there for you to help guide you to the next step no matter what that next step happens to be as long as you remain open to it.

---

[17]   See Chapter 6, "Doing the Work".

Chapter 9

Business 101

The following chapter is not a comprehensive guide to owning your own business. There are plenty of books and classes that will provide you with a much better overview on general business principles than this chapter. Rather, what these next sections contain are what SPIRIT and I believe are the most important elements to building a business for energetic healing practitioners. Feel free to skim this chapter and only pull out the pieces you need or skip it altogether if you like if you think you already understand the basics.

The Balancing of Many Hats

If you have spent the majority of your professional life working at a medium to large company, you are accustomed to doing only one or two single tasks and doing them all day long. Whether you were a clerk in a busy office or a line worker in a factory, your skill set was generally limited to one or two basic functions and when it came time to punch out at the end of the day, there was no need to think about what the other moving parts in the business were doing. If that describes you, you are in for a very big change!

Being the owner of your own business requires you to perform the functions of an entire group of office specialists, all while working to meet the needs of your clients. Most new entrepreneurs do not have a lot of money to invest in their new venture, so if you do not know how to do something, you are going to need to learn how to do it on your own. Thankfully, YouTube and websites like Skillshare are affordable ways to give yourself a crash course in the basics of what you need to know, when you need to know it. If you do not have a college degree in Business Administration, do not think you have to get one, but you should consult with someone who has a business degree whenever you come across something you do not understand.

Generally, most entrepreneurs spend a quarter of their time generating income, and the other three quarters of their time doing the administrative tasks they need to do in order to generate more income. The time to learn how to do the mundane things you are going to need to know is at the beginning of your practice. In the beginning, your client load may still be light enough where you are generating a nominal amount of cash flow, but you still have plenty of time in your day to figure out what to do with it. Below are the five "Hats" you will need to wear as the owner of your own healing practice:

Hat #1: The Boss/CEO. As the head of your own business, you are the boss. If you have always had a boss in the past or if you have ever been the boss or manager at a place you worked, you know that the boss is in charge of making sure that everything is running according to schedule. If something is not going right, it is the boss's job to fix it. If somebody calls out sick, it is the boss's job to make sure that the job still gets done. If somebody does not know how to do their job, it is the boss's job to make sure they get trained. Even if you are your only employee, one of those people needs to be the boss!

Hat #2: The Accountant/CFO. The Accountant's job is to make sure that all income and expenses are properly recorded, and that all invoices and bills are paid. It is their job to make sure that all receipts and inventories are properly accounted for and preserved. It is also the Accountant's job to make sure that all financial documents are filed with the proper authorities on time. They make sure that the taxes you owe are properly calculated, filed and paid on time. The Accountant needs to be able to let the boss know at any time whether the business is making a profit, treading water, or sinking to the bottom of the ocean.

Hat #3: Office Manager/COO. The Office Manager's job is to make sure that all scheduling and client paperwork is in order. It is their job to schedule and re-schedule clients, fill out important paperwork like business licenses, occupancy certificates, insurance forms, and whatever else comes across their desk. They are also in charge of keeping up with Continuing Education Credit requirements, answering emails, returning phone calls and text messages to clients and vendors, ordering supplies, and making sure that the office is clean and professional-looking at all times.

Hat #4: Marketing Director. The Marketing Director's job is to let the world know that your business exists and to convince them to come out and give you a try. They are in charge of building your website, establishing your "brand", ordering marketing materials, scheduling public appearances, networking with other practitioners and organizations, writing your blog, producing your YouTube Channel and engaging social media.[18]

---

[18]   You need to be careful of this one. They like to spend money you may not have!

Hat #5: Healer. The Healer's job is to engage with the client and work to address whatever it is they need help with. The Healer has absolutely no idea how to run the business nor do they care very much. Their first and only priority is to their client and their client's well-being. The Healer works to help their client heal by doing research, attending additional trainings, and by meditating and taking good care of themselves at all times.

If you join a group practice, it is possible that one or more of these roles will be assigned to the main owner or maybe even to a professional receptionist or Office Manager. However, you need to keep in mind that Hat #1 for your business always belongs to you, no matter how many other practitioners are working at the group practice.

This may sound impossible at first, but with time, patience, and a constant connection to High Self, you should be just fine! Remember that you are going to make plenty of mistakes and sometimes those mistakes are going to cost you money. As long as you are doing your best and you are not deliberately trying to break the law, 99% of all mistakes will be forgiven.

Branding & Marketing

You will make your Marketing Director very happy if you choose a consistent brand that will be able to adapt and grow with you over time. Your brand is how you will be introducing yourself to the world and it needs to not only express who you are and what you do, but it also needs to encourage potential clients to try you.

There are five elements to a strong brand.

1) A strong brand is clear on its mission and purpose. It is motivated by your core values and convictions and what drives you to do this type of work.

2) A strong brand understands and leverages its uniqueness. You are a unique person and so is your business. You are a specialist in your field and clients are drawn to you because of what you bring to the table. Your brand needs to reflect that uniqueness.

3) A strong brand is clear on its target market. What type of person is your typical client? Are you the type of healer who wants to work with high-powered CEOs and captains of their industry, or are you looking to attract housewives and soccer moms? Your brand needs to speak to who you want to be treating as a client.

4) A strong brand maintains a consistent on-brand message. However you communicate while using your brand, whether it is on your website, social media, or press releases, your brand must remain consistent to your core values at all times. NEVER use your work email or Facebook page to post ANYTHING that is inconsistent with you being the most positive, loving healer you can possibly be. All it takes is one negative post to go viral and you will be forced to re-brand your business and start all over again!

5) A strong brand continues to build solid relationships with its community. If you are running a Facebook page, how quickly to you respond to comments on your posts? If you are posting a blog, how consistently to you post new material? If you are making a personal appearance, where you are answering questions in a live forum, are your responses positive, clear, and connected to High Self? If your community sees you as being consistently responsive and positive, future clients will see that and make contact with you.

If you are not confident that you can build a strong brand yourself, this is a task you may want to outsource to a professional. If you are concerned about how much a professional may cost, consider this – How much will it cost you to re-brand your business because you got it wrong the first time? Other marketing tips include:

1) Do not do anything that makes you uncomfortable. If public speaking is not your thing, take a Public Speaking class or do not book public appearances where you will need to speak in public. If you hate to travel, keep your travel radius to within half a day's drive so you can go home at the end of the engagement. Understand your personal limitations and adjust your marketing plan accordingly.

2) Proofread everything! Check all marketing materials for typos, spelling errors, grammar, etc. BEFORE it goes to the printer! Your printer will not re-print an entire stack of brochures for free because you spelled your own name wrong.

3) Make it FABULOUS! If you cannot make your marketing materials look like it came from a professional office, do not put it out into the world. Business cards and brochures should not look like they came from your home printer. If you are producing a YouTube channel, invest in some professional equipment (i.e. camera, lighting, microphone, editing software) and know how to use it. If you are buying furniture for your office from a thrift shop, clean it up to make it look as new and professional as possible.

4) Look the part you are playing. Whether you are making a professional appearance, seeing clients at the office, or

simply going to the grocery store to pick up some milk, you are the personification of your brand. Whatever it is you want that projection to the public to be, you need to keep it consistent every time you leave the house because you never know who you are going to run into when you go out. The more clients you see, the higher the probability you will bump into them on the street or in the market. Further, treat every encounter with a client or stranger as a potential opportunity to book another appointment at your practice.

The bottom line when it comes to promoting your brand is that your marketing materials and how you present yourself is the "face" of your brand. After all, when the business consists of you and nobody else, you become the embodied personification of your brand. Therefore, your brand must not only be attractive to potential clients and consistent for your existing clients, but it needs to already be such a strong part of who you are that you will be able to wear it effortlessly every day.

Accounting & Taxes

You do not need to have an accounting degree or be a tax professional in order to be able to keep track of your revenues and expenses. However, if you fail to keep accurate track of your business finances, it is likely that you will end up paying too much in taxes at the end of the year. Alternatively, you may discover that you did not pay enough and you owe more in taxes than you anticipated, or you may end up owing back taxes and/or interest and penalties. As the business owner, you are responsible for making sure that your finances are in order, yet most new entrepreneurs are generally clueless about how to do that.

Choosing a business entity. If you own the business by yourself or you own the business with your spouse, you are a Sole Proprietor. What this means is that your personal finances and your business finances are generally mixed up together and when you file your taxes at the end of the year, you will be completing a Schedule C, which is attached to your standard 1040 tax return. The Schedule C can be confusing to fill out so you should seek the assistance of a tax professional to help you.

If you own the business along with another practitioner who not related to you, you are a Partnership. What this means is that even though you should have a separate bank account for the business, the two of you are still personally on the hook for any expenses the business has. When it comes time to file your tax return, you will need to file TWO returns, one for the Partnership and the other for yourself. The Partnership return is a Form 1065, which should be prepared by a tax professional.[19] For your personal taxes, you will receive a Form K-1, which tells you how much of the Partnership's income you need to count in your personal income tax return.

What to Count. The Internal Revenue Service allows you to deduct legitimate business expenses from what you owe in Federal Income taxes, but what is counted and not counted in state income taxes varies from state to state. If something you pay for or buy for the business is *Reasonable and Necessary* for the continued operation of the business, then it is a legitimate business expense. If the expense is not *Reasonable and Necessary*, it is not. The following is a list of expenses that are generally considered *Reasonable and Necessary* when operating a small business:

---

[19]   Important Note: If you need to file a Partnership (1065) Return, the deadline to file in the United States is March 15th, NOT April 15th.

Advertising (includes website, direct marketing, etc.)	Bank Fees for Credit Card Transactions	Training and Education (CEU's)
Dues & Subscriptions	Travel Expenses (Special Rules Apply)[20]	Entertainment (50%)[21]
Business-related Insurance	Legal and Professional Fees	General Office Expenses
Sales and Property Taxes Paid	Postage	Office Rent
Supplies	Business Telephone (and/or cellphone)[22]	Contracted Labor
Office Utilities[23]	Wages to Employees	Cost of Goods Sold[24]

If you pay for an out-of-pocket health insurance plan, retirement fund (IRA) or health savings account, those are

---

[20] Consult with your Accountant or Tax Professional.

[21] Entertainment expenses (such as dinner at a restaurant) can be counted at a 50% rate (which means only half of the cost of the dinner can be counted) if the purpose of the dinner was to discuss business or to bring in new business. For example, dinner with a client or a vendor to discuss a new revenue stream or to convince the client to send more business your way can be counted, but dinner with your friend who happens to be a client cannot be counted. The IRS looks at Entertainment expenses very carefully when they do an audit, so for this category, always follow the adage "when in doubt, leave it out!"

[22] If you have a cell phone that you use for both business and personal use, make a reasonable estimation of how much you use the phone for each and only count the expense that you believe reasonably represents your legitimate business use.

[23] For Utilities in a Home Office, use the percentage of square footage that the office occupies against the total square footage of the property.

[24] See the "Managing Inventory" section below.

NOT counted as business expenses on your Schedule C. You count those expenses elsewhere on your Income Tax return, so you should still keep track of them, but do not count them in your business records.

How to count it. Some people prefer to purchase accounting software like QuickBooks for Business, or some other software program with pre-set categories and tax-related calculations, but these programs can be expensive and often require training to know how to use them. The value of purchasing a software package verses simply keeping everything on a spreadsheet comes down to how complicated your business is. If your only sources of revenue are client fees, and you only have a few expense categories, there is no need to buy accounting software. If your revenue sources are coming from multiple places, (i.e. client fees, book royalties and/or merchandise sales) or if you have complex expense categories, (i.e. employee wages, expensive equipment inventories, and/or long-term debt) then buying accounting software and/or hiring a Certified Public Accountant (CPA) will be in your best interest.

Understanding Net Income. When you receive your paycheck from your employer, your pay stub lets you know how much money you earned during the pay period. It then itemizes the money your employer withheld from your paycheck for taxes, health insurance, 401K, etc., and at the bottom it tells you what your "net paycheck" is. Net Income works the same way. You add up all of the fees you collected from clients, and then you subtract out all of your business expenses and what you have left is your Net Income.

Managing Inventory. Many SRT Practitioners like to sell pendulums and other items they buy at wholesale or make themselves. This is a great way to make a little extra cash when you go to psychic fairs or host trainings, but you need to treat the expense and sale of pendulums differently than how you treat client fees. Whether you make your inventory yourself or you buy them from a wholesaler, you cannot count what you pay for your inventory as a normal expense. You can only count what you paid for them AFTER you have sold them.

For example, let us say that you spent $20 on supplies to make 10 pendulums. The $20 does not get counted as a regular expense. Instead it goes on a separate spreadsheet as the value of your inventory. On your inventory spreadsheet, you have an inventory of 10 pendulums valued at $2 each ($20 divided by 10). Let us say that you sell two pendulums at $10 apiece. On your inventory spreadsheet, you now have 8 pendulums valued at $2 each for a total inventory of $16. On your income and expense spreadsheet, you would count $20 of revenue from sales of inventory, and an expense of $4 called "Cost of Goods Sold". If you sold the entire inventory, you would count $100 in revenue, $20 in Cost of Goods Sold, and the value of your current inventory would be $0.

In addition, most states and some municipalities require that merchants who sell certain types of goods to the public must pay sales tax. Further, where the sales tax must be paid depends on where the sale took place[25], so if you are selling your goods at a psychic fair in another state, for example, you will need to pay sales tax to the state where the sale took place. For a while, sales of goods sold over the Internet were not subject to sales tax, but those laws are changing depending on where you happen to live. Check with your state's tax authority before you make your first sale because most states require all vendors to register with their state tax office and fill out monthly or quarterly sales tax returns, even if they had no sales

---

[25]   This is often referred to as the "Point of Sale".

during a given period.[26] Service fees from clients are generally not subject to sales tax, but that may vary depending on where you live. Always check with your local tax authority before you begin taking money from clients

Other Accounting Tips. Below is a list of best practices that will make your life (and your Accountant's life) a lot easier when it comes time to file your income taxes.

- Keep all receipts. What I do is I put all of my receipts into a binder and organize it according to category. Your Accountant or tax professional is likely to kiss you for that!

- Count everything you can. If you have a home office that you use exclusively for working with clients, you can count some of the rental value and utilities expense for that space as a regular business expense even though you did not make a specific payment to your landlord or utility company for it. Your tax professional or Accountant has specific forms that will help you make those calculations.

- Keep track of unusual mileage expenses. If you are traveling somewhere to attend a special event that is outside of your normal commute to and from the office, you can count the number of miles multiplied by the IRS's current mileage rate (minus your normal commute) as a regular business expense. You cannot count your normal commute to and from your primary

---

[26] Be sure to add filing your state sales tax return to your monthly "to do" list because many states will charge a penalty for not filing a return even if you did not owe any tax!

place of business, no matter how far away it is from your house.

- Reconcile monthly. Be sure to reconcile your finances on a monthly basis. Not only will this allow you to get a quick snapshot of how you are doing, it will give you a good idea if the quarterly income taxes you are paying to the IRS are too much or too little. Some practitioners like to wait until they file their taxes in the spring before knowing how much they owe in taxes and they suddenly find themselves owing more than they can afford to pay at the time. By estimating your monthly Net Income based on your prior year's Net Income and reconciling that on a monthly basis, you will end up owing a lot less to the government when it comes time for you to file your taxes. Further, you will have a lot more peace of mind when you go to sit down with your tax preparer.

I am sure that the preceding chapter is missing something important pertaining to your particular business, but I hope I have provided you with some of the basics that will allow you to get things started. As we stated in the beginning of the chapter, as the owner of the business, there is an expectation that you understand how to run your business or at least know what questions to ask if you do not. The best advice I can give any new entrepreneur whether they are an SRT Practitioner or any other type of healer is to keep excellent records of everything you do and if you get stuck on anything at all, or you think you do not know how to do something, do not be afraid to ask a professional for help.

Chapter 10

Unlocking Abundance & Gratitude

So you have opened your practice, you have cleared all of the energetic blocks that were preventing you from taking this leap of faith, you have your office, an awesome brand, and your books are perfect. You have started to see clients, and you are doing good work. However, when you look at your monthly financial statements you are seeing that you are just breaking even. You are managing to make enough money to pay your bills and stay open, but you are not making enough to take a vacation, attend that workshop you really want to attend. You may also be worried that you do not have enough money in the bank where if your client load suddenly drops, you may not be able to pay all of your bills.

What is going on?

For the past five-thousand years, humanity sees itself from a paradigm of scarcity that for some of us, is very difficult to break. Since the beginning of recorded history, the majority of people have been in a constant condition of slavery, serfdom, which led to industrial wage slavery. While our culture has propagated the illusion that anyone can get rich if they work hard enough, the reality is that the majority of the world's population lives in poverty while only the top five-percent possess true abundance in their lives. This has conditioned many of us to be satisfied with the condition of barely scraping by while the so-called ruling classes enjoy all the abundance for themselves.

Unblocking Abundance

SPIRIT informs me that while we are conditioned to equate success with mere survival, we imagine that those who have abundance in their lives have achieved some level of "perfection" (Chart 8a), which creates "emotional impingements" (Chart 28) in ourselves that prevent us from welcoming abundance into our own lives. Indeed, SPIRIT goes on by saying that we have "reservations to expanding consciousness once Universal God Consciousness is attained" (Chart 22) because we believe that we are somehow undeserving of reaching the next level of consciousness, which is to welcome the abundance we deserve into our lives.

In order to bring abundance into our lives, SPIRIT informs me that we must take on the soul qualities of "Composure and Benevolence" (Chart 2), which is much easier said than done. In addition to clearing any energetic programs or blocks to these soul qualities, welcoming abundance requires additional life changes to break the hundreds of lifetimes we have had where we felt undeserving of anything more than just getting by.

The first step is by reducing or eliminating negativity in your life and that begins by switching off the news, or reducing it to a mere trickle. No matter where you stand on the political spectrum, bad news surrounds and penetrates us from all sides. It is in our social media feeds, it is on the television, it is in the newspapers, it is on magazine covers at the grocery store, it is on the coffee table at your dentist office, it is on the monitors at the airport and the gym, and it is even on the television screens at your favorite restaurant. When we see bad news, it automatically creates an energetic condition in our subconscious of scarcity and fear. We fear that whatever bad thing is happening in the news will somehow affect us directly and we feel scarcity to where we want to hold on tighter to what we have, even if what we have is not so good for us!

We have to remember that the job of the news media is to reinforce the paradigm that we live in a dualistic world of a physical reality. Duality believes that there is "good" and "evil" in the world, and that you are always on the side of "good" and everyone else is on the side of "evil". If you have gotten this far into this book, you already know that duality is an illusion. The ego creates and reinforces it in order to prevent us from connecting to SOURCE energy. So if the news media's job is to keep us from connection with SOURCE, why are we paying attention to it?

Shut Off the Feed

Below are some strategies to cut the news media from your subconscious mind:

- Turn off your TV. Better yet, if you have cable or satellite television, cancel your subscription and stick with Internet-only service and an al-a-carte television streaming service like Amazon's Fire Stick. That way you can select which channels you watch and not have to pay for the channels you do not watch.

- Monitor your emotions. When watching a television show, movie, or any other type of entertainment, take a moment and watch the person watching the show. Is the person watching the show feeling relaxed or anxious? Are they learning something positive about themselves, or are they learning to hate or distrust? If the person watching the show is somehow diminished emotionally or energetically by the act of being entertained, then that person (you) needs to turn it off or walk away.

- Cancel all magazine subscriptions that contain negative media. If you are not sure which ones do or do not, use the pendulum to help you decide.

- "Unfollow" social media friends who consistently post bad news from the media. Personal issues are okay as long as they are not the type of person who posts every negative emotion they happen to feel throughout the day. You do not need to "unfriend" them so they can still see your posts and they can still contact you directly if they want, but unfollowing them will remove their negativity from your news feed. "Unfriend" social media friends who are openly hostile, racist, and are otherwise intentionally negative.

- When traveling, bring something to read or listen to that is empowering, and ignore whatever is happening on the TV monitors. This also applies when you go to the gym or while you are waiting at your doctor's office.

- When not "on the clock", avoid answering email, text messages and phone calls, even from clients. Exceptions can be made for times when a client is truly in crisis, but 95% of the time, your time to rest, relax and/or spend time with your loved ones is time you need to recharge your batteries so you can operate at your very best. When you react to an email or text message that could have waited, you are acting from a place of scarcity and fear, and not from abundance.

Cutting negativity also applies to what books and stories we read, the video games we play and what movies and television shows we like to watch. When considering whether a piece of media is good for us, use your pendulum to help you decide. Some of the most popular entertainment franchises in the world are also the most negative. Sometimes we can learn something from watching something that we find disturbing, but most often, it only brings our energy down to a lower frequency, which reinforces our energetic programs of fear and scarcity. Use your pendulum to help you decide what is best for you and ignore the rest.

Another way to remove negativity in your life is to avoid hearsay and gossip whenever possible. Not only are personal stories that are from second and/or third hand sources rarely true, they are often intended to be harmful to the person being spoken about. It does not matter whether the subject of the gossip is the Queen of England or your next door neighbor; gossip is simply another form of negative energy that we need to cut out of our lives.

You will be surprised at how much better you will start feeling about yourself and the world around you once you have eliminated the negative wire feed into your subconscious. Many people are afraid that if they cut off the feed that they will miss something "important" that is going on in the world.

This is something that I used to believe, so I conducted an experiment to test that theory. What I did was I shut myself off from all news media for a month, which was hard for me to do because I was a person who would spend 2-3 hours a day reading and/or watching news programs.

As a former history teacher, I was constantly on the lookout for so-called "tipping points", and teachable moments, so I would view every news item from as many points of view I could find in order to get a better understanding of what I believed to be the complete picture. At first, it was hard not to click on my favorite news sites. The inner need to know what was going on so I can say "I told you so" to anyone who would listen was almost overwhelming! To my total amazement, I looked back at my old media feeds a month later and absolutely nothing had changed. The same madness was still going on in the world, the same disasters were still happening, and the same commentators and talking heads were preaching the same doom and gloom they were talking about the previous month. Yes, some of the details were different, but the "news" was still the same. The other interesting thing that happened was how I started to feel when looking at my old "reliable" sources. I felt sick to my stomach as if I just swallowed a poisoned pill thinking it was medicine!

The other amazing thing that happened was that my client load suddenly increased. It was like I had broadcasted to the Universe that I was no longer drowning in negativity, so now I was in a place mentally and energetically to actually help my clients with whatever they were going through. The "news" is not part of my life any more, and since then arguments with my family are less frequent, my son actually wants to spend time with me, and I am feeling more intimately closer to my wife than I have felt in years!

Accept Who You Are

The next step to finding abundance is to accept yourself for whomever or whatever you are. This can be hard for some of us to do because on a deep level, many of us do not have a positive view of ourselves. We have already provided strategies on building a more positive view of who you are in Chapters 5 and 6, so we will not repeat those strategies here.

Marla Goldberg[27] is an SRT Consultant, Healer, Intuitive, Author, Speaker and host of Guided Spirit Conversations podcast (mghealer.com). When she first learned about SRT, she was going through a very difficult divorce with her first husband. While most divorce proceedings are settled informally between attorneys, Marla's ex-husband took the case to trial intending to intimidate his wife into a weaker settlement.

Marla had just started seeing her SRT Practitioner on a regular basis, and even though she did not see an immediate change in herself, her outward energy started to shift. Her own lawyer noticed it, but more importantly, her ex-husband's lawyers and the judge noticed the change in energy. By the time the final gavel sounded, Marla was able to balance the negative energies thrown at her so that she could begin her new life and leave the past behind her.

One of the things we learn as we work with SPIRIT is that the only person who can harm us is ourselves. The other souls in our lives are a reflection of the bliss and/or turmoil we have chosen to experience in this lifetime, and we have the power to choose whether those reflections are helpful or harmful. Through the SRT work, Marla started to see herself

---

[27] Marla Goldberg's story was provided with permission from the source. For more information about Marla's energetic healing practice, please visit her website.

as the light and the love of the Universe, and the people who were working against her started to see that as well. That is why that no matter how much her ex-husband wanted to hurt her, the people around him were unable to follow through with his plans.

By taking the SRT clearings and practices to heart, it becomes easier to accept yourself as the guiding light of the Universe that you were intended to be. If you can accept it and believe it, others will come to believe it as well, and so will your clients.

Unblocking Gratitude

Part of bringing both spiritual and financial abundance into our lives is to be truly grateful for those gifts when we receive them. We can connect many of our blocks to gratitude to our blocks for abundance, but SPIRIT informs me that this is not always the case.

When we think about a child who is ungrateful, we imagine that a young person who has all the food, shelter, love and attention that they need, but are unable to truly appreciate those gifts because they have never experienced their absence. So a parent will sometime take away some of the things that a child has taken for granted in an effort to teach them a lesson to have more gratitude for what they have. This type of lesson never works because all we are actually teaching our children is that we give love in direct proportion to the amount of gratitude and appreciation we express to it. Gratitude does not work this way.

Gratitude, at least how it is connected to the health and well-being of your healing practice, is as much a "dysfunction of Creative Energy" (Chart 15) as much as it is a block to abundance in general. Your healing practice is supposed to be the fountain of your maximum creative energy. You created this practice with the guidance of High Self in order to help facilitate humanity's ascension to SOURCE, so it makes sense that if you are having trouble being "open to receive greater good" (Chart 21) on behalf of yourself and your clients, then that would hinder your practice's ability to thrive.

According to the Mayan and Vedic Calendar, about five-thousand years ago, our civilization entered an epoch where we define our physical existence by its separation from SOURCE. The epoch that is passing was the "Age of Pieces" and the new, more enlightened age is the "Age of Aquarius". The Vedic refer to this current age as the "Iron Age", and that the new age we are entering is a new "Golden Age". As we close out this current epoch and we enter into the new one, we must remember that we are but the "Embryo" (Chart 29), the ultimate potential of all that can be, as we start to reach out and embrace the new paradigm of "Understanding and Love" (Chart 2).

Ancient mythology tells us that during the last Golden Age, humanity had a civilization that we can scarcely imagine today. That civilization built the Great Pyramids, the ancient ruins at Machu Picchu and the city of Atlantis. The inhabitants of those cities were able to move and carve great stones without machinery because perhaps their connection to SOURCE allowed them to manipulate matter on the subatomic level the same way we can heal ourselves by bending reality to our intension. That golden civilization met a cataclysmic end what followed was our current civilization. A civilization characterized by duality, greed, and ego. The Mayans refer to time as a great wheel, so now it is starting to come around again to a new golden age, and you and I are part of humanity's new connection to SPIRIT.

The next time you sit for your daily meditation[28], and you alert your consciousness to connect to SPIRIT, set your intention to receive all of the understanding and pure love that SOURCE can provide because now the door is open to all of us. As you imagine yourself standing at the foot of the Great Golden Light of all that was and all that will ever be, recognize that you are but the embryo of humanity's new ascension. As the embryo of a child absorbs all of the nourishment and love that a mother can provide, be like an embryo of spirit ready to absorb all of the nourishment and love from SOURCE. SOURCE energy is a never-ending, abundant flow of light and energy. It knows nothing of scarcity or lack. It knows who you are from the beginning of time to your soul's ultimate ascension back to the GRAND I WHOLE, and it loves and understands you unconditionally and completely. Feel that love enter into your entire being, and you will know Gratitude!

To accept that gift from SOURCE is to embody what it is to express Gratitude. By holding on to that feeling of gratitude from the Universe, you will become the beacon that will allow your practice to experience abundance and thrive!

---

[28]   See Chapter 5.

Chapter 11

Integrating and Expanding Your SRT Practice

As your personal healing practice begins to grow, it is going to evolve over time. While the Spiritual Response Association (SRA) offers several additional healing modalities that were developed by Robert Detzler and others within the SRA, chances are you are going to find your practice evolving according to your own interests and advancing skills as a healer. You may find that being a "healer" is not even your highest calling!

As with any other profession, as an energetic healer, you are going to have good days and bad days. You are going to have clients who are going to transform before your eyes and you are going to have clients that you cannot help. SPIRIT reminds us that no matter what types of clients come our way, that you always find ways to "enjoy" (Chart 19) working with your clients as you continue to seek ways to expand your "understanding and love" (Chart 2) with them.

Whether you decide to work exclusively as an SRT Practitioner or if you decide to branch out into other healing modalities as your practice starts to grow, SPIRIT reminds us that "learning is a continual process" (Chart 27) where you are constantly seeking ways to expand your own consciousness back to SOURCE. For that purpose, the Spiritual Response Association (SRA) is continually offering certification programs and elective courses to assist you on your journey. While the SRA does offer SRT Practitioners with a prescribed path through vetted and approved training materials, your path is still your own. Your ultimate goal is to learn ways to serve your clients, and there are hundreds of ways you can go about doing that outside of the traditional SRT certification programs.

Becoming a Certified SRT Consultant

After you have been practicing SRT for a while, you may be ready to take the next step and become a Certified SRT Consultant. The SRA certifies all Consultants while also maintaining a database spanning the globe. Each Consultant pays an annual membership fee and must complete additional training beyond the Basic and Advanced classes.

Currently, all Certified SRT Consultants are required to take the "SRT Intensive Skills" class in order to apply for their certification for the first time. They must also take this class a second time within the first two years in order to renew their certification. This is a three-day class where you review the SRT skills you learned in the Basic and Advanced classes, plus any new information and/or protocols. At the end of the class, the Teacher tests each student to demonstrate their ability to do a full clearing plus two other specific protocols.

Being a Certified Consultant allows you to be included on the SRA's website directory so that potential clients may be able to find you, and you have access to all of the new learning opportunities being offered through the SRA. In addition, you have the ability to volunteer or otherwise assist the SRT community to help spread SRT to the world.

Before you decide if becoming a Certified Consultant is right for you, you should first consult High Self before scheduling your first Intensive Skills class. If you are uncertain, contact your SRT Teacher and ask them to ask High Self on your behalf. Some SRT Practitioners can be quite successful at running their own practices without official certification. However, if High Self is guiding you to seek the certification so that you can be in a better position to help bring SRT to the world, then you should also ask High Self to help you provide the means (both financial and spiritual) to do so. (See Chapter 10)

Whether you decide to become a Certified SRT Consultant or not, your Basic and Advanced SRT education does allow you to enhance and grow your practice by taking further trainings that have been sanctioned by the SRA.

Self-Mastery (SR) is a class that is required for any SRT Consultant to take their practice to the next step and become an SRT Teacher. This is a two-day class that is followed by a three-month learning schedule with periodic group/mentoring meetings.

Spiritual Restructuring (SpR) is a unique system developed by Robert Detzler that is designed to bring together the spiritual and physical aspects in a holistic healing system. It bypasses your conscious mind and taps into the cellular memory and wisdom of the body using bodywork, muscle testing, and using the pendulum. This is a six or seven-day class that is only open to SRT Practitioners who have taken the Basic SRT class. You must take SpR in person, so scheduling and travel is a factor when it comes to taking this training. Although the SRA does not specifically sponsor SpR classes, many SRT Teachers also practice and teach SpR as part of their overall healing practice.

Spiritual Healing is a book and healing program of healing symbols channeled by Robert Detzler to help clients suffering from acute and chronic illnesses. It provides expanded instructions on how to use Chart 7 and the "Healing Circle" chart, but the book's focus is to provide you with downloaded symbols that can be infused into a client's energetic field to apply direct healing for a vast number of different illnesses and conditions.

Many SRT Practitioners, whether they are Certified Consultants or not, use the additional training opportunities described above to grow and expand their practice for their clients. Whether you choose to incorporate these other healing methods into your practice is a matter of personal taste, availability of resources, and whether you are being guided by High Self to expand your practice in this manner. Some practitioners like to have many tools at their disposal so they can be prepared for many different types of situations while other practitioners prefer to do only one thing and do it well. You may even come to realize that SRT is not your tool of choice at all, but that you only want to use it to complement and enhance another career choice altogether.

Other Paths to Integration and Expansion

If becoming a Certified SRT Consultant or Teacher is not in your destiny, or the thought of sitting down with clients to help them clear their programs does not sound like your calling, you can still integrate what you have learned from your SRT training into other healing and non-healing modalities.[29]

What some former SRT Practitioners do is they continue to do "clearings" for their clients, but they either allow High Self to help them write up new charts or they abandon the use of the charts altogether. Some former SRT practitioners use muscle testing instead of the pendulum, and some practitioners use nothing at all but their "belief" and increased "awareness" (Chart 6b) of their connection to High Self. SPIRIT informs me that whenever incorporating SRT into your regular healing practice or if you decide to set off on your own and blaze a new trail, you must "guarantee that everything is clear" (Chart 25) before proceeding. As long as High Self guides your decision and you have confirmation that High Self and not ego guide what you are doing, then you have permission from the Universe to proceed.

In addition to doing "clearings" on clients, there are literally hundreds of other complementary spiritual healing modalities, certification programs, and educational opportunities that exist outside the SRT world. So if you are not feeling called to work exclusively with SRT, you can simply use it as an additional tool in your toolbox when working with your clients. Examples of other complementary modalities include:

- Spiritual Life Coach
- Family Therapist / Psychologist

---

[29] Just remember that if you are not following the SRT method, you cannot call it SRT. Additionally, you are prohibited from teaching and/or distributing copyrighted training materials to anyone who is not an SRT Practitioner as all training materials are protected by copyright, which is held by the SRA. This is done in order to protect the integrity of the SRT protocols and to ensure that anyone who is receiving SRT training is provided with consistent information that has been sanctioned by the SRA.

- Minister / Justice of the Peace
- Financial Counselor
- Shaman
- Acupuncturist / Herbalist
- Chiropractor / Osteopathic Physician
- Massage Therapist / Reiki Practitioner / Body Worker
- Social Worker
- Holistic Medical Doctor / Family Medicine / Nurse Practitioner

And the list goes on and on! The primary benefit to integrating SRT into another practice is that you can increase your "sensitivity to others' energy" (Chart 17), which will allow you to be a more affective healer no matter what your primary healing modality happens to be. If you are working in a career in which helping people is your primary focus, you can integrate SRT into your practice!

The Path of Integration

If you are a healing practitioner who wants to use SRT as an additional service to a service you already provide to your clients, you can incorporate SRT in one of two ways. The first way is to use it as a stand-alone value-added service to your clients, and the second way is to use SRT to aid you in your treatment research for your client.

Let us say that you are a licensed Psychologist or Family Therapist. Your clients are primarily individuals and/or families in crisis and you have a number of tools available to you in order to help them address their needs. You may offer SRT as an additional value-added service to those clients who can be helped by the clearing of their soul records. However, you must explain to your client that SRT is outside of the mainstream of recommended therapy methods, and if they choose to proceed with the service, it will appear as a separate item on their bill, which may not be covered by their health insurance carrier.

Something else that some therapists have done is they use SRT when conducting group therapy sessions in order to clear the room of any discordant energies prior to bringing in clients for the session, and again once the session is over in order to help clear the energies that were brought up during the session.

As a Financial Advisor, your job is to help your clients plan for retirement and provide for their families through wealth management. Most Financial Advisors use standard investment and diversity strategies that are rather generic depending on the level of risk tolerance of the client, and yet some clients will do very well while other clients will not. You can use SRT to help clear your clients' programs surrounding money and to help them attract more abundance into their lives. You can either do this as a value-added service or you can simply do this on your own as a standard service to all your clients.

SRT as a Research Tool

You can incorporate SRT research methods into other healing and non-healing modalities as well. For example, let us say that you are a medical doctor or nurse practitioner. You are presented with a challenging case where the conventional protocols of your profession are not making the level of progress you would like to see, or the patient is presenting with symptoms that could point to any one of a number of different possible treatment options, but you are unclear as to which treatment you should pursue first.

The first thing you should do is ask permission from the patient's High Self if you can research their soul records to help you find the best treatment option for them. If you get an affirmative, then proceed to clear out any emotional blocks or programs that are preventing the patient from receiving the maximum benefit from their treatment. Reduce the influence of your ego to less than 3% and then check with High Self to help you pick the right treatment option. Seek confirmation of the choice to 100% from High Self, and then confirm with the tools of your trade to ensure that a properly documented justification for the treatment you have chosen is included in the patient's medical record.[30]

If you are unclear as to whether the treatment chosen by High Self is the right choice, again, seek confirmation to 100% and ensure that you have reduced your ego to less than 3%. If everything checks out and there is no medically rational reason not to proceed, move forward with the procedure and trust that High Self has guided you in the right direction.

The first time you try this method might be to be a little frightening. The physical world and your professional medical training teaches you to approach each patient with such a degree of scientific medical detachment that releasing the ego and saying to the Universe "I don't know the answer", is contrary to everything you have been taught in medical school. So trusting that SPIRIT knows best can be a scary prospect for the ego. To make this work, you need to temporarily put down your training and trust that the Universe and High Self knows more than you do when it comes to healing your patient. After

---

[30]   Nobody needs to know that you carry a pendulum in your pocket. As long as the treatment chosen by High Self is medically sound and gets the desired result, nobody is going to care how you reached that conclusion!

all, your patient has placed all their trust in you to make them feel better, so if you are at a loss about exactly how to do that, then you need to trust that High Self will be there to help you as long as you ask for it. Once you have your answer from High Self, feel free to put back on your doctor's uniform and proceed as though you knew exactly what you were doing all along.

Other applications of the SRT research and clearing methods include:

- Helping police officers and detectives when working to solve complex cases;
- Helping real estate agents to remove Separates and other disincarnates from houses they are trying to sell or they can use SRT to help clear their clients so they can remove the blocks from finding their new perfect home;
- Helping Search & Rescue responders look for survivors after a disaster if other methods are unavailable or unreliable;
- Helping hikers find fresh water, or help them find the safest way across a dangerous stretch of trail.

As long as High Self is guiding you and you do not allow your ego to control the swing of the pendulum, the possibilities for the different applications for this healing technology into your life and your career are endless. The key to allowing SPIRIT to guide your life is to "let go of the old" (Chart 19) where the ego dictates how we make our decisions in life, and embrace a new paradigm where you are a channel for SOURCE energy that is guided by High Self.

PART III

DOING THE WORK

Chapter 12

Compassion for the Stubborn

In this final section of this book, we will discuss some of the more challenging clients and situations you are likely to encounter as an SRT Healer. As much as we would like to attract those clients who are willing to do the work to bring about positive changes in their lives, more likely than not, you are going to encounter clients who will be a challenge for you emotionally and energetically. This is especially true for those clients who have been suffering from chronic conditions and/or life-threatening illnesses.

What you must always remind yourself when you go into work each day is that your clients are coming to you for a reason. You are the amalgamation of a lifetime of training and life experiences that is unique to you and you alone. Therefore, you should be attracting to you only those clients who you can actually help, whether it looks that way or not.

The Importance of Compassion

I have a client who tests the limits of my compassion; we will call "D". D is a woman in her late 60's who has been coming to see me for several months, but despite multiple SRT sessions, D's main complaints have not significantly improved. Her physical and emotional symptoms go through periods of acute relief, but then she experiences a relapse of symptoms soon afterward. Every time I feel like we are starting to make progress, she comes back to see me the following week and her complaints are often the same as they were the previous week. Sometimes they have even gotten worse!

Whenever you encounter a client that you feel you are unable to help despite multiple sessions, it may be a case where you and the client have some negative energy between you. Before deciding to end the client relationship, you should first research whether there are any discordant programs between you and the client that is preventing any healing from taking place. It is possible that you and your client have a shared past life together where a program or contract was put into place that is preventing you from doing your work with them. If all of the programs are clear, it is also possible that you and your client are simply not a good fit for each other. If High Self indicates that your client would be better suited for another practitioner, turn to your healing community[31] and ask High Self if someone in your community would be a better fit. If someone in your community is not a better fit for your client, then you should ask High Self to guide you to a practitioner outside of your healing community.

When you want to refer your client to another practitioner and you have confirmation from High Self that this is the right

---

[31] See Chapter 7 – Building Your Healing Community

thing to do, you need to take the next step and actually facilitate the referral. When referring a client to another practitioner, it is important that you communicate with that practitioner as to the reasons why you feel they are in a better position to help your client and ask them what they need from you to facilitate a smooth transition. Some receiving practitioners want to know as much detail as you can provide, while others want to know as little as possible so they can diagnose your client without prejudice. Once the referral is complete, in most cases, your client is no longer your client. That means you are not entitled to ANY diagnostic or treatment information from the new practitioner unless your former client has granted specific and written permission to do so.

Even when referring a client is the right thing to do, some practitioners decide to hold onto a client because they are afraid of letting them go. Some practitioners are afraid that if they refer a client out that other practitioners will see them as weak, or otherwise unable to take care of their clients. You may be afraid of losing a stream of revenue from a client you need to refer. Others fear that if they refer a client to another practitioner, the other practitioner needs to somehow reciprocate and refer one of their clients to them, or the other practitioner somehow "owes" them something. All of these things are ego-driven nonsense that has nothing to do with the well-being of the client, and everything to do with the ego of the practitioner. If you are finding yourself thinking any of these thoughts before referring your client to another practitioner, be sure to clear them before you do anything else.

So what happens when you want to refer your client to another practitioner, but High Self indicates that you are still the best practitioner for them despite your apparent lack of progress and frustration? Again, that is when you need to remind yourself that you and your client were drawn together for a reason, and even if that reason is not clearly apparent to either one of you, you need to trust that SPIRIT knows what it is doing!

After several sessions of what I perceived as a clear lack of progress, I wanted to refer D to a different practitioner, but D did not want to see anyone else. D told me that I was the only practitioner who ever made her feel any better about herself, even if it was only temporary. When I consulted with High Self, it indicated that D selected me for a reason, and even though D was a frustrating client to work with, she was making progress and that I needed to continue working with her.

We often need to remind ourselves that a healer's best Soul Qualities (Chart 2) are "Unity", and "Compassion", but those qualities can sometimes be blocked by "guilt" (Chart 8b) when we encounter clients who suffer from an "Unwillingness to Learn" (Chart 17).

Clients who challenge the limits of our compassion are a normal part of the work we do, but we also must remind ourselves that we have all undergone periods in our lives where we refused to listen to good advice, even when someone we trusted gave the advice. We have all experienced times in our lives when a parent, teacher, or even a stranger gave us sage advice that we wholeheartedly rejected because our egos were preventing us from listening to what they had to say. There have been times in my life where I even paid for professional advice that I completely rejected. Therefore, as the practitioner, I can understand how challenging it can be to accept payment from a client who I perceive is rejecting the service I am providing.

When a client pays us the fee for the work we do, but we feel like no progress is being made, it can start to make us feel guilty for taking their money. Society places an unrealistic expectation on all service providers. The idea is that if we are exchanging money for a service, then some sort of quantifiable outcome must be the result. Further, there is a belief that if there is no measurable result, then the client is entitled so some sort of refund because we have somehow failed to heal them. When it comes to this type of work, nothing can be further from the truth!

Whether it is through the Western medical model or something on the esoteric scale, the healing arts does not come with a money-back guarantee. If your doctor tells you that you have cancer, does that mean you get your money back if whatever treatments your doctor recommends fails to stop the cancer and you die? Of course not! Your doctor will do their very best to provide you with the best care possible, and in return, you and/or your insurance company will compensate them for their efforts. If it were your time to die despite their best efforts, it would be unfair to say that your doctor failed you.

This is not the same thing as malpractice. Malpractice occurs when your doctor failed to provide their best effort to treat you or they made an avoidable error that made your condition worse. As long as you follow your training and you follow the SRA's code of ethics, failing to make someone better is not grounds for anyone suing you for malpractice. Your job as the healer is to help facilitate the healing process in your client. You have done your job if you provide the best advice you can give in accordance with the training you received. Your client has the free will to choose whether they will take that advice but whether they make that choice is not your responsibility. That responsibility lands solely on your client.

If you are feeling any sort of guilt because you are not making the level of progress with this client that you may have seen in other clients, all you are really feeling is your ego, and not High Self. Remember that your ego is firmly planted in the dualistic paradigm of existence, and so it is easily caught up in the trappings of the rules of cause and effect, which we already know are merely an illusion. If the work you are doing is coming from a place of compassion that is guided by High Self, then the work is good and you are entitled to any agreed upon exchange for those services.

You are going to encounter clients like D. That is a simple fact of the work we do, so prepare yourself for when that happens. Whenever you encounter a client like D, do the work by making sure that all of our High Self Committees are aligned and so are our client's, and that our ego has been reduced to under 3%. It is also very important that right from the beginning we explain to our clients that progress is not always visible or measurable. Oftentimes the work occurs "behind the scenes" in the SPIRIT realms, which are not always immediately measurable here on the physical plane.

We often forget that despite our connection to High Self, our clients still have free will. One of the last things I tell my own clients is that although we have opened the door to a better life by clearing away the programs they have built throughout their lifetimes; it is still up to them to walk through that door! If they refuse to walk through that door because their ego is too strong, it is not your fault because you did a bad job clearing their programs. It could just mean that they have more programs to clear or it could mean that their souls are just not ready to shed the ego to the point where they can take that first step.

How We Measure Progress

As healers, we are tempted to measure the progress of our client's healing based on the perceived relief of the symptoms they came to you to work on. For example, if a client comes to you because they are experiencing chronic back pain, we are tempted to measure their progress based on how much we reduce their back pain. If a client comes to you because they are having problems in their relationship with their partner, we are tempted to measure their progress based on how much better the client and their partner are getting along. SPIRIT does not work that way.

"Progress" does not work on anyone's timetable that we invent for ourselves. "J" is a male in his late 40's who was a referral from another healer in my network. The referring practitioner warned me from the beginning that J is very impatient and was "looking for a miracle". J suffered from chronic back pain that medical science and a long line of energy healers could do nothing to eliminate. The first thing I told J was that the work we do does not work on anybody's timetable. I went on to explain that the work we do often works with subtle energies that can open the door for healing and the relief of symptoms, but that actual physical relief of symptoms can take time, and often occurs in ways that we least expect. Apparently, J did not hear me. He apparently had somewhere he needed to be by the end of the following week and it was very important to him to have significant relief from his symptoms at that time. So when the following week came and went and J did not experience the results he was looking for, J was disappointed.

As I hope you have seen in the work you have done on yourself up to this point, SPIRIT not only asks us to change our bad habits, but SPIRIT also can ask us change our careers, our relationships and how we view the world in order to live our best lives so that we can live lives in freedom. Both D and J would often fight me on this point because all they really wanted was to return to a time in their lives when they were free of the discomfort they were feeling but to continue to live their lives in the same manner that created their pain in the first place! I would tell them that their expectation to be "healed" without doing any of the work is a lot like drinking poison and expecting someone else to die! During their sessions, I would tell them what SPIRIT recommends for them to change their lives for the better, and often their answers would be "no", or "that's too hard", or simply "can't you just tell SPIRIT to make things the way it used to be?" There is not a lot you can do about that except to remind them that it is very difficult to move forward when all you are doing is looking behind you, and hope that some of that wisdom eventually starts to sink in.

It is extremely important that when our sessions fail to meet our client's expectations, that we remind and counsel them that SPIRIT does not work according to our expectations, but rather it works for the client's highest good. The energies that we work with when we do SRT are often subtle, sometimes dramatic, and never what we expect to see. If a sudden, miraculous relief of physical pain is in the client's highest good, then that is what we are likely to see. If the pain is there to teach a soul about the value of compassion and mercy, then no matter how many sessions or physical interventions the client experiences, their pain will remain until their soul has accepted that lesson, which could be in this lifetime, or it may even be in another lifetime.

Therefore, we should measure progress based on the wisdom the client has received within their sessions, and how they start to integrate that wisdom into their lives. For this, we often have to check in with High Self. In both D and J's cases, I checked with High Self to determine how much progress they were making in terms of the wisdom they were integrating. To my pleasant surprise, both clients were doing extremely well at holding onto the clearings we had done despite the fact that the sessions failed to meet their ego-driven expectations.

Dis-ease is a Gift

I often we tell my clients that whatever dis-ease they are experiencing is a gift from SPIRIT. Debilitating pain, personal tragedy, life-threatening injury, and even a terminal diagnosis is the Universe's way of telling you to stop and listen to the messages it is trying to tell you. We already know that this lifetime is not your first, and it is unlikely that it is your last. If you fail to listen to the Universe this time, you will get another opportunity to listen again in another lifetime. The people you know (and sometimes envy) who live supposedly "charmed" lives where nothing tragic or painful ever seems to happen to them are generally not in this lifetime to learn very much. Perhaps they learned their lessons in a previous life, or perhaps they will learn their more dramatic lessons in another lifetime. Eventually, we all are faced with circumstances that force us to step away from the ego and reach out to the Divine for help, guidance and healing. If this is your time for a dramatic lesson, you need to take that opportunity to learn and grow from it.

By informing my clients that their pain is the Universe telling them that they need to open their souls in a more connected way of living to the love of SOURCE, it provides them with a context that they may not have received from anyone else. Although this can be difficult at first for our clients to hear, the deeper we go into the work of allowing the messages of High Self to come through, the more we are able to allow the healing to take place. Things may never go back to the way it was when they were able to live in ignorance and be free of their pain at the same time, but why would we want that for them? What we want is for their souls to be enlightened so they will not experience the same level of suffering they are experiencing in the next lifetime. We can help facilitate the integration of that wisdom in order to relieve their suffering, but if it is in the client's highest good to endure that suffering in this lifetime, it is not up to us to judge that soul's conscious decision.

Your Client is You

Our clients are our greatest teachers. The client who refuses to listen to High Self may be a message from High Self to tell you to be a better listener. The client who refuses to change their diet may be a message from High Self that you need to re-examine your own diet. The client who is constantly looking back to happier times when they were younger may be a message that you must also learn to leave the past in the past and to treat each new day like the best new day of your life!

All souls belong to the collective consciousness that make up the flow of the Universe. Therefore, on a soul/energetic level, we are ALL ONE. Your client is you and you are your client! The more patience and compassion you can feel for your all of your clients will increase your ability to feel more patience and compassion for yourself!

Chapter 13

Challenging Cases

As we alluded to in the previous chapter, not all of your clients are going to be easy cases or easy people to work with. Again, we must remind ourselves that the reason why each of our clients chose to come to us and not someone else is that on an energetic level, their soul group and/or their High Self Committee decided that you had something to offer that they may not have been able to find somewhere else. So if you are faced with a case that you think may be out of your depth or experience level, remind yourself of that fact, and proceed as if God had guided your client directly to your practice because you have something special to offer.

"E" was a big man in his late fifties who loved to be outdoors but he suffered from chronic pain for the past thirty years and despite surgeries, medication, and countless hours of physical therapy, he never saw any relief. A friend of his referred him to me, so he figured he would try it. In his first appointment he told me flat out that he thought what I did was "voodoo crap" that was not going to work, but since his friend agreed to pay for the first few sessions, he thought he would give it a try.

Generally, I do not have a lot of hope for clients like this when they walk in the door. If they come back for a second appointment at all that is a small miracle in itself. SPIRIT informs me that there are some clients that are so cut off from SOURCE energy that they become blind to the possibility that anything can help them. "Demonic Forces" (Chart 5) block these clients. When we talk about Demonic Forces in this context, we are not talking about pointy-headed imps spawned from the Underworld. What we are actually talking about is a complete and total disconnection from SOURCE so that all is left is the ego.

Clients like E come to me generally because someone referred them, as they generally do not come of their own volition. "M" is a female in her late 30's who came to see me because her friend made her promise to give me a try because they could see that M was not feeling any better despite months of various therapies and treatments from other practitioners. Like E, M suffered from the "Demonic Forces" block on Chart 5, which was preventing her from making any sort of connection to SOURCE energy.

Whenever we encounter clients like this, the first thing we must do is we must remove the block that is causing the disconnection. In the case of E, I removed the energetic block without his conscious knowledge because High Self informed me that there would be greater energetic resistance if he knew what I was attempting. In the case of M, we spent a good amount of time in the very beginning going through each step of the Prep to Work in order to break down the resistance of her disconnection so that way we could finally break through it.

Once we remove the blocks, then the hard work begins as we now have to re-train the client's soul to be a recipient of SOURCE energy. For that, we need to convince the soul to express a "willingness to change" (Chart 19) an entire lifetime's worth of habits where the ego was calling all the shots. SPIRIT informs me that we generally need to turn to Chart 32 (Check List) in order to begin our negotiations with the soul to accept change in their current lives. Specifically, we turn to "Alpha to Omega" clearing, "Heart Energies" and "Psychic Wounds".

Alpha to Omega

When we do an Alpha to Omega clearing, we turn to Chart 3 and we work our way down the chart and then back up again until we can raise the soul consciousness to the new paradigm above RADIANT LOVE. This is because clients who are failing to see any results from the treatments and healing sessions they received suffer from a soul consciousness that is firmly planted in the physical plane of existence. By raising the level of soul consciousness above RADIANT LOVE, what we are providing the soul is a perspective that is above the physical.

Much like the parable of the blind men and the elephant, where five blind men were placed on different parts of an elephant and then were asked to describe it, when the soul consciousness is only aware of one aspect of its existence, it starts to believe that only one small part constitutes the whole. Just as the foot or the trunk of an elephant fails to describe the entire beast, only a single aspect of one lifetime hardly constitutes the sum of a soul's entire existence! By providing the soul the perspective that this lifetime is merely a moment in a cosmic lifetime, the problems of this life become smaller and much more manageable.

As we advance the soul consciousness to each rung of the ladder on Chart 3, clients who suffer from a strong disconnection from SOURCE tend to be stuck, especially on the incarnation levels. It is as if the soul is trying to climb a treacherous mountain, but they insist on taking the contents of their house along with them, including the "kitchen sink". As they reach each gateway, the guardian at the door tells them to let go of things they brought with them and allow them to fall away off the mountain. If they refuse to let go of their "things", or they try to convince the guardian that their possessions are too important, they will be denied entry to the next level.

As your client's soul consciousness gets stuck at each level on Chart 3, work to clear the programs that are preventing the soul from letting go of their burdens. Once the soul is able to let go of the things that were holding it back, move onto the next place where the soul is stuck, and then work to clear those programs as well. Do not stop until your client's soul consciousness has been elevated to the New Paradigm above RADIANT LOVE, and then receive a 100% guarantee from the soul that its consciousness will remain on that level. Ask if a Brain Restructuring or an Inner Child Progression will help once the soul is elevated, and if you get an affirmative response, follow the protocol accordingly.

Heart Energies

The program referred to as "Heart Energy" occurs on the "King of Kings", "Queen of Life" and "Lord of Lords" levels on Chart 3. It is on this level of the soul's evolution where it begins as an entity indistinguishable from SOURCE and then it evolves into something more like an individual that is distinct and different from other entities. At this point, the soul is infused with both positive and negative words, which are designed to guide the soul into its incarnation cycle. While the soul consciousness is in the Garden of Eden, the words have no effect. However, once the soul has eaten of the "tree of the knowledge of good and evil" and has begun their incarnation cycle, the words start to exert their influence.

The Tree as described in the Book of Genesis, is the metaphor for the dualistic existence, which is the basis of our physical and spiritual incarnations below the King of Kings level of soul consciousness on Chart 3, and it is the root of our own slavery to its ideas that some people are "good" and others are "evil". The "words", which are the basis of the Heart Energies, are the chains of our own enslavement to this idea. The prejudices we assign to all people, plants and animals on this plane of existence can be found in those "words". Since the words were infused into our souls prior to our incarnation, they are firmly rooted beliefs that cannot be simply changed just because we decide to change our minds.

Robert says that it is not necessary to learn each positive and negative word that were infused into the soul at this level, but to simply clear the influence of those words on the client's soul programs. In other words, we cannot simply erase these words like we can erase a program in a client's soul records, but we can reduce their influence by elevating the soul to a level of consciousness as if they were again standing within the Garden of Eden and the words have no meaning.

Psychic Wounds

Greek mythology tells the tale of Chiron, the Centaur. Chiron was the son of Philyra, a beautiful sea-nymph and the Titan, Cronos (called Saturn by the Romans). So beautiful was

Philyra that Cronos took it upon himself to stalk and rape the unspoiled nymph. To hide himself from his searching wife, Rhea, Cronos disguised himself as a horse while he continued his foul deed. Philyra soon gave birth to a half-man/half-horse and despite her sweet disposition, the memory of her assault prevented her from ever loving the child. So rather than live with her disgrace, Zeus granted her wish to transform her into a linden tree, where she would continue to provide beekeepers with sweet honey but provide no sweetness for her own son.

Despite being without parents to care for him, Chiron was one of the gentlest of all Centaurs who was famous for his wisdom and knowledge of medicine. He went on to tutor many famous Greek heroes including Heracles, Achilles, Jason, and Asclepius. Despite his wise and gentle nature, Chiron continued to suffer throughout his life from the betrayal of Cronos and the rejection of Philyra, to the point where he was constantly putting himself into harm's way in order to influence the course of humanity's development through his use medicine and his mentorship of both mortals and demi-gods. His sense of self-loathing and self-sacrifice was so great that when a poisoned arrow cast from the bow drawn by the demi-god Hercules shot him, he chose to renounce his own immortality and was placed among the stars as the constellation Centaurus.

The myth of Chiron serves as a cautionary tale of how certain souls, when granted the ability to act as co-creators of the Universe, can sometimes abuse that power which can inflict a Psychic Wound. Psychic Wounds are the inflicted scars of the soul when a particularly powerful soul does something to another soul that is inconsistent with the divine plan. The wounds are generally of a deep and personal nature where a powerfully trusted entity abused that trust to satisfy their own narcissistic needs.

The perpetrator of the Psychic Wound is generally an advanced soul who has some degree of ability to act as a co-creator in the Universe, but who is still susceptible to the temptations to satisfy the ego. They are generally attracted to souls who possess the qualities of "Innocence" and "Patience" (Chart 2) and so they use their creative power to inflict harm on those souls, which takes the form of a Psychic Wound, which will then follow both souls throughout many lifetimes, both past and future. I have also found that the perpetrator of the Psychic Wound can be an aspect of the client's own soul due to some sort of error programming at the GODHEAD or I AM Level on Chart 3.[32]

The problem with Psychic Wounds is that they are usually self-replicating due their traumatic nature. Just as the person who suffers from post-traumatic stress becomes more deeply stressed each time they recall the original traumatic event, whenever we work to clear a Psychic Wound without also seeking to reconcile the parties involved, the wound will often simply reappear. However, after it reappears, it will come with another layer of energy around it in order to protect itself from further interference, which will make it more difficult to clear again.

When our souls first became distinct entities separate from SOURCE, it provided itself with an individual Soul Package containing the lessons of existence. The intent of the Soul

---

[32] This is an extremely rare instance where an aspect of the creator soul is left behind on the Spirit Realm yet continues to inflict harm on the incarnated soul on the physical plane. The solution is to attempt merge both aspects of the soul so that they become "whole" again and then to reconcile any discordant energies that may have resulted due to the split.

Package is to bring it back to SOURCE once we learn all its lessons. However, as entities with free will, we are all still susceptible to succumbing to the will of the ego, which is embodiment of separation from SOURCE.

So why would an advanced entity with the power to co-create aspects of the Universe decide to abuse that power by succumbing to the power of the ego? SPIRIT informs me that these souls suffer from a "Loss of Subconscious Integrity" (Chart 10a) whereby they become disconnected to SOURCE, and yet they maintain their abilities to be co-creators nonetheless. Indeed, ancient mythology is populated by many such advanced entities like Cronos who gave in to their physical desires while remaining extremely powerful and creative beings.

Psychic Wounds can affect all lifetimes and all dimensions as they are part of what we call "Infinity Programs" (Chart 29), which ripple and affect the victim's soul throughout all time and space. Psychic Wounds can sometimes manifest physically as tumors, cancers, birth defects, and genetic mutations. They can also manifest as phobias, mental illnesses, so-called "phantom" pains, or illnesses where symptoms are present, but a physical cause cannot be found. If the original wound was particularly violent in nature, it can also manifest in a present life experience of the same violent act or trauma repeating itself lifetime after lifetime.

If we identify a Psychic Wound during the mop-up process, clearing it is relatively easy as we simply need to ask High Self to clear all Psychic Wounds at all levels, and to receive assurance that they are 100% clear. However, if Psychic Wounds are the root cause of your client's physical or emotional inability to heal, then a more direct approach may be necessary.

The treatment of Psychic Wounds can be an extremely delicate procedure as the issues surrounding the infliction of the original wound may be manifesting in the present life as well as past lives. In our own practice, Nina and I employ both shamanic soul retrieval protocols along with SRT in order to convince our client's soul to not only allow the wounds to heal, but to also forgive the entity who inflicted the wound in the first place. In order to do that, we need to elevate the soul of both the perpetrator and the victim so they can recognize that they are both children of SOURCE, and that within SOURCE, there is no room for anger, hate and pain, but only unlimited love and acceptance. If we are successful, then the client's soul will gain the ability to accept the healing energy that we are bringing to it. If we are unsuccessful, we know that our next attempt will be more difficult than the last.

Not all of your clients will be challenging ones, but they will show up from time to time. Oftentimes, your clients are your best teachers as they will challenge your faith in High Self and force you to think outside of the box of our physical existence. When challenging clients present themselves to you, do not be afraid to think outside of Robert's charts and protocols if High Self is guiding you somewhere else. Robert designed his ideas and frameworks to be just that, a framework to help you to help your client facilitate the real healing that goes beyond the confines of the SRA publications.

Chapter 14

Miracles Happen

When you do this work long enough, you will be a witness to some genuine, Jesus-level miracles. Most of the time, the miracles we help to facilitate are on the smaller scale, but sometimes you get to see something that will completely change your mind about everything you ever thought you knew to be real.

The reason why we refer to miracles as being miraculous events is due to their ability to defy our belief systems as to what is real and what is not real. When a person suffering from stage four cancer goes into remission, we call it a miracle because almost everyone at this stage only has weeks to live, which is hardly enough time to make the complete life change necessary for something like that to happen, and yet people have managed to do it. When a yogi is able to levitate into the air or stop their breathing for hours at a time without harming themselves, we call it a miracle because we believe that gravity and breath are universal constants that make no exceptions for us mere mortals, and yet we have no explanation even when we see it happen before our eyes.

I find that miracles are possible when you think about what the physical Universe is actually made of. On the surface, we see the world around us as being this solid mass of physicality that is hard to create, and nearly impossible to put back together once destroyed. When we look at our hand, what we see is this solid thing on the end of our arm, but when you look closer, you see a thing that is made up of various tissues, bones, blood and cells. When you look even closer inside each cell, you see nuclei and cell organelles. When you look closer, you see DNA and chromosomes. Look even closer and you see molecules and atoms. Look even closer than that and what you see is... space! Lots and lots of space between protons, neutrons and electrons that are all simply bound together by invisible strings of entangled energy. Further, science has demonstrated that these subatomic particles can be moved and manipulated by our very thoughts and beliefs over any distance faster than the speed of light! If we take those entangled energetic particles and blow them up back into this thing we call a hand, we can finally wrap our brains around this notion that the entire Universe is simply an illusion that can be moved and changed based on our thoughts and beliefs alone. Therefore, this illusion of illness and dis-ease can be manipulated, changed and healed just so long as we believe it to be possible and we can tap into the Universal Light Energy of SOURCE.

Some people say that miracles never happen because they have never seen one, when the truth is that miracles happen every day as long as you know how to look for them. One of the things we ask our clients to do is we tell them to keep a "miracle journal" so that they can see for themselves the miraculous things that happen in their lives and how their positive and negative beliefs influence the events in our lives. The key to attracting miracles in your life is to set your intention as directed by High Self, and then to increase your awareness of how the Universe brings the miraculous things into your life whether you are conscious of it or not.

When miracles happen with our clients or when they simply happen in the world, our human belief systems automatically seek an outside cause or reason for why this happened. The person cured of cancer must have been misdiagnosed, or the yogi must be employing some sort of optical illusion or that you must have somehow hallucinated or dreamed the experience. [33]

Another temptation we have when it comes to miracles is that we want to assign some sort of credit for it. When the believer who goes to the faith healer or prays upon the apparition of the Virgin Mary and their injuries and illnesses are suddenly healed, we want to assign the credit to the healer or the event. However, if that is the case, why do some people experience a miracle, but other people who see the same healer experience no "cure" for their condition?

R is a male in his late thirties who suffered from a variety of symptoms that he believed stemmed from the fact that he contracted Lyme's Disease as a youth. He went to see several doctors and specialists from all over the country and they were unable to find a cause for his recurring symptoms, which would flare up especially during times of acute stress. When I saw him, High Self indicated that he had no disease, and he was in perfect health, but that his symptoms were the product of a system of beliefs that he had built up over several lifetimes. Further, we discovered that if he did nothing to clear those beliefs, his symptoms would get worse until they

---

[33]   In Chapter 6 I described my experience with healing my own diagnosis through the power of belief, which led me to alternative healing practices until there was no trace of the condition in my latest blood test.

manifested into an actual physical condition that would require medical intervention. When our beliefs manifest into a physical condition, it becomes a lot harder to "unbelieve" them, because our minds have a very hard time getting past this physical "thing" in our bodies that now have a presence we can see, feel and touch. Whether that thing is cancer, arthritis, or any number of chronic conditions we can think of, once our minds can sense it with our five senses, it has taken on a physical reality that can be nearly impossible for most of us to let go. We attempted to clear the programs surrounding his belief that he was sick over the course of several sessions, but after each session, his symptoms would return because his belief in his illness was stronger than his belief in his ability to clear it.

After R decided to stop seeing me, he learned about a faith healer in Europe who was famous of removing several lifetimes' worth of pain and suffering from the people she saw, often in only one or two sessions. So R booked a flight to Europe to see this faith healer because he was convinced that she would succeed at "healing" him, where I could not. The irony is that after he saw this woman for two sessions, she told him the same thing I told him during our SRT sessions, and while she was able to provide him temporary relief from some of his issues, he did not receive the "miracle" he was looking for. Eventually, all of the relief he experienced from the healer in Europe was gone and he was right back to how he was feeling before.

S is a male in his late forties who suffered with back pain from the time he was fifteen years old. S came to me because he heard that SRT could help, but he had no expectations one way or the other. He believed, however, that his pain was connected to the death of his father who died about the same time that the pain began. After clearing the guilt and the burden he felt when he had to assume the role his father left behind, the pain was miraculously gone after only two sessions!

So why was S able to receive his miracle while R could not? Both clients were about the same age and in about the same physical health. Both practiced meditation on a regular basis and both of them took the time to be sure they ate the right foods, took the right supplements, and got the same amount of exercise.

The first thing we must always remind ourselves is that the miracle of healing is never the doing of the healer. As the healer, you are the facilitator and the teacher, but you are not the one who is actually doing any of the healing. The healing comes from within the client. If the client is not 100% committed to taking responsibility for their own healing, then no miracle will ever happen.

If you ever spent some time on a busy casino floor among the slot machines, you will see a certain type of person always hovering around the edges of the floor. This person is carefully watching for which machines are "winners" and which ones where gamblers walk away with empty coin cups. Their expectation is that the machines that tend to reward their players more may win more often, but the payout will be less, and the machines that tend to rob their players will win less often, but the reward will be much higher. These players are "shopping for a miracle", with the belief that if they choose carefully enough, that one special machine will provide the miracle they are looking for, as long as they choose the right one.

The truth of the matter is that almost all slot machines are programed with an algorithm that sets the odds of winning with each pull of the lever. Just as with each throw of the dice the odds of landing on a particular number is the same no matter how many times you throw them, the odds of hitting a jackpot on a particular slot machine remains the same no matter how many times you pull the lever. Yet there are people who consistently leave the casino with more money than they came in with, and there are people who consistently leave the casino with less. So is it the machine making the miracle, or is it the person pulling the lever?

Just as the slot machine is programed with the ability to reward or not reward with the same odds with each pull, the healer is programed with certain training, advice, and protocols that are designed to work the same way with each client, no matter who they are when they walk in. Therefore, the straight odds that your client will walk away with the right treatment or advice to facilitate a miracle are the same as every other client who sees you, and since the odds are always stacked in favor of the house, more likely than not, your client will be walking away feeling no different than how they walked in. The only difference is that the client who is ready to energetically take responsibility for their own healing process is the one most likely to experience the miracle, and the client who is looking to you to make the miracle happen for them will probably walk away disappointed.

SPIRIT informs me that one of the greatest "challenges" (Chart 25) of the healer is to understand that they are not the healer at all, and sometimes they are not even the facilitator of the healing. Sometimes, they just happen to be a witness to the healing when it actually takes place! Some healers believe that their ability to facilitate miracles stems from a certain familial lineage or ethnic background, commonly referred to as "race beliefs" (Chart 10a). You need to remember that any belief you may have about your ability to be the healer needs to be cleared because any such belief is just part of the illusion. SOURCE recognizes no one soul to be any more or less special than any other soul, so if you believe that your legitimacy as a healer stems from your training, ancestry or any other factor, this is just a product of your ego and therefore, it is not real. The "root cause" (Chart 31) of all miraculous healing, both big and small, belongs to the person being healed and their connection to SOURCE, and not to you.

In the previous chapter, we were introduced to E, a male veteran in his late fifties who was suffering from chronic debilitating pain for over 30 years. E had seen countless doctors, surgeons, physical therapists, and even a psychiatrist but in all cases, he did not see any relief from his pain. When he came to see me for the first time, E was very skeptical that anything would be able to help him and he was not afraid to say so. E was not looking for a miracle because he believed that miracles did not exist.

After we covertly cleared E's disconnection to SOURCE energy, E's affect started to shift to where he started to talk a little more about his life. Just like with S in the example above, SPIRIT uncovered that E's pain was connected to an emotional trauma he experienced about 30 years ago that had nothing to do with his physical pain. The more we talked and cleared his emotional issues, the more E started to open up and trust me. To everyone's surprise, his pain started to subside. Eventually, he was virtually pain free to the point where he can now mow his lawn and take walks in the woods without needing to sit down and take his pain medication.

E's recovery was a miracle, but who was responsible for the miracle? Was I the miracle-worker because I recognized that all E needed to heal from his pain was to feel listened to, or was E the miracle worker because he was able to allow himself to open up to another human being and trust that he would not be hurt? Was it possible for E to recover from his pain if

I recognized what he needed but E was unable to allow it to happen?

In the previous chapter, we were also introduced to M, a female client in her late thirties who suffered from migraine headaches, depression, anxiety, and a whole host of other conditions, which made it very difficult for her to live her life. M was referred to me by one of her friends in the hope that we could clear some of the programs that were preventing her from seeing any relief from her chronic symptoms. After clearing her disconnection from SOURCE through a step by step application of the Prep to Work, we spent most of the rest of the session clearing past life traumas that were affecting her present life.

I only saw M once. While she found the experience to be profound, a part of her was too comfortable being "sick", so she asked that we not continue with our sessions. Despite her desire to return to the way things were before, her other care providers noticed an immediate change in M's affect after she saw me. Her treatments became a little more effective, her mood swings were less pronounced, and her migraines were less intense, which was miraculous in itself because M had been stuck in the same rut for a number of years.

So even though M did not experience a complete recovery, what we were able to do was to convince her High Self that a recovery was a possibility, which did not exist before. While M is still not in a place where a complete recovery can happen, her subconscious has been provided a glimpse of a possibility of recovery, which is a lot more than what she ever believed was ever possible. Will she now take the next step and continue to walk down that road? That is entirely up to her. All I do know is that if she decides to walk down that road with me or anyone else, her new connection to High Self will now help make that possible.

In Chapter 12 we were introduced to a client named J. J came to me expecting a miracle to happen. Like the wallflower at the casino, J was looking for healers with a proven record of accomplishment of performing "miracles" for their clients. When a former client experienced a miraculous recovery from tennis elbow, they told J that I was a "miracle worker". J suffered from chronic back pain for several years where a long line of doctors, physical therapists, and energy workers were unable to provide any relief from his symptoms. A friend recommended that J should see a psychotherapist who specialized in this type of emotional pain, but that practitioner was very expensive, and so J was seeking a more affordable (and miraculous) alternative. J was tired and desperate for immediate relief and before the session even began, and so right out of the gate J wanted to know when he could expect to see some relief.

So what do you do with a client who comes to you expecting you to do all the work to facilitate their miracle? As we explain in Chapter 12, when you first sit down with clients like this, you need to explain and counsel them about how we must rid ourselves of any expectations that any miraculous healing is going to take place, and the work we do does not come with a money-back guarantee. As we already know, J did not listen to me, and so J could not help but be disappointed when relief from his symptoms did not happen.

Despite the fact that J did not get the miracle he was looking for, J and I continued the work for several more sessions over the course of about three weeks. We worked on releasing blocks to healing, Inner Child Progression, Alpha to Omega, and we followed all that up with Brain Restructuring. After doing just about every SRT protocol in the book, the one thing we could not do was relieve any of J's physical pain, and so we agreed that it would probably not help to see each other for another session. Interestingly enough, the miracle with J happened after we were finished with our final session. Since J no longer had the burden of the expectation that I would provide him with any miracle, he were able to let his guard down and begin to allow the healing to finally start to make a difference in his life.

While J's physical symptoms did not go away, J started to see his pain as the teacher it was as he began to explore other avenues and possibilities in his life. Rather than seeing the pain as an obstacle, he started to see it as an opportunity for growth. As we learned in Chapter 6, the path of true healing always begins with the self. What J started to realize was that his pain was telling him to "Lower his Energetic Shields", to continue to "Do the Work on a Daily Basis", and to "Commit himself to a Journey of Self-Discovery" so that he could someday find his joy. J is also starting to understand that healing comes from within, and so he decided to take a break from "healers" for a while so he could take a good hard look at his own life.

Even though I am no longer seeing J on a professional basis, J still sends me an email every now and then to let me know how he is doing. He still has good days and bad days, but lately the good days are starting to outnumber the bad ones, and considering where J was before he started to see me, I would call that a miracle in itself!

Conclusion

It is my sincere hope that you have found the preceding chapters helpful in your journey to be an SRT healer. Please keep in mind that I have based the experiences and advice in this book on my own experiences and my connection with SPIRIT, and your own experiences will likely be quite different from my own. Also, keep in mind that some of the specific advice in this book may change due to changes in law, SRA policies, and/or new guidance from SPIRIT. We all have this tendency to hold onto the written words we find in books as if written in stone, when in fact, they can be as fluid as the waters of the ocean.

If there are any parting words of advice I can give that will provide encouragement as you take your first steps on a journey that will change your life forever, it is this. Never stop listening to what SPIRIT is trying to say to you. The Universe WANTS you to be successful and prosperous. Humanity needs you to be the best healer you can possibly be!

Be well and let your light shine forth!

Thank you, SPIRIT!

Printed in the United States
By Bookmasters